COLOGNE

Make the most of your time!

VISIT THE CITY

BKB Verlag

COLOGNE AT A GLANCE

3 Days in

- The Old Town
- Cologne in the Evening
- Romanesque Churches
- Shopping and Strolling
- Along the Rhine
- Art Museums
- Cathedral

Content

LEGEND

- X Duration of the tour
- ◆ Opening times/ departure times
- ▲ Transport stop
- ➤ see

© BKB Verlag
All rights reserved
1/19

Editor:
Dr Brigitte Hintzen-Bohlen

Layout:
Andreas Ossig
BKB Verlag GmbH
www.bkb-kommunikation.de

German-English translation:
John Sykes

Printing:
Brandt GmbH, Bonn

ISBN 978-3-940914-64-4

All contents and information
have been conscientiously
researched and carefully che-
cked. Nevertheless it is not
always possible to avoid errors
entirely. We are therefore
pleased to receive corrections
and proposals for additions.

BKB Verlag GmbH
Auerstrasse 4
50733 Köln
Telephone 0221/9521460
Fax   0221/5626446
www.bkb-verlag.de
mail@bkb-verlag.de

Welcome to

... a city of a million people on the Rhine, famous for art, Carnival and Catholicism. It was the most important place of trade in the north of the Roman Empire, in the Middle Ages a leading European city thanks to holy relics and commercial privileges, and today Cologne is Germany's fourth-largest city, a centre for media and international trade fairs, a business hub in the west, a university city and a lively location for art and culture.

More than 2,000 years of history have made their mark on Cologne: Romans, archbishops, merchants, French and Prussian rulers have all left their traces. Unique in the world are the twelve Romanesque

Cologne ...

churches. The Old Town with its little lanes is picturesque, the cathedral a World Heritage site, and the museums are outstanding.

In addition to many sights, numerous events attract visitors from all over the world – whether they come for Carnival or Christopher Street Day, Lit.Cologne, the Comedy Festival, Gamescom, Art Cologne or the Christmas markets, they can experience the Rhinelanders' love of life all year round.

In contrast to other large cities, this "village" of a million residents on the Rhine has never lost its homely character. This has a lot to do with the many different quarters ("Veedel" in Cologne dialect), where locals feel at home, and with the mentality of the people, who say that "Cologne is a feeling" and feel warm at heart when they glimpse the two towers of the cathedral. The people of Cologne love their city, have a more relaxed attitude than residents of many other places, and don't always take things too seriously. This mix of light-heartedness and lethargy, tolerance and ignorance, big-city atmosphere and small-town idyll, cultural highlights and imperfections in urban planning make Cologne such a lovable place ...

About Cologne

● Cologne has its own "code of law", a wonderful description in the local dialect (called Kölsch) of the mentality here. The first two articles express a fatalistic attitude to life: "Et es wie et es" ("Things are as they are") and "Et kütt wie et kütt" ("What happens, happens") because, as the third article states "Et hätt noch emmer joot jejange" ("Things have always turned out well").

● The phenomenon known today as "networking", i.e. making contacts to cultivate mutual interests, is known as "Klüngeln" in Cologne, and the city has long worked on the principle of "you scratch my back, and I'll scratch yours". Those who went to the same school, or are members of the same sports club or Carnival association, naturally stick together.

● Cologne has become the leading media city in Germany. Six major TV channels, including the commercial RTL and the public WDR, as well as four radio channels, are broadcast from Cologne. A third of nationally screened TV productions, TV films, daily soaps, game shows and talk shows, including the leading talent show and "Who Wants to be a Millionaire?", are made in Cologne.

● Cologne University was founded in 1388 and is one of the oldest in Europe. It was, however, closed in 1798 under French occupation, and

did not open again until 1919 as the "new university in Cologne".

● As long ago as 1516 Cologne's brewers began to protect their local speciality, a light-coloured, top-fermented beer, by establishing rules and obeying the German laws on purity. They renewed this in 1986 by signing the Kölsch Convention, a voluntary agreement of the brewers of Cologne beer, called "Kölsch".

● Cologne-Bonn Airport has the only runway in Germany that is also an emergency landing site for the NASA space shuttle.

● From 1880 to 1894 Cologne Cathedral was the world's tallest building. At 157 metres it is the second-highest church in Europe.

● For almost 60 years Europe's first suspended cable car has taken passengers 900 metres across the Rhine between the zoo and Rhein-

park, which was also opened for the Federal Garden Show in 1957.

● Cologne's prominent citizens are buried in the Melaten cemetery, which contains some 55,000 graves and is at the same time a nature reserve, home to many kinds of plants, squirrels, bats and more than 40 species of birds and insects.

● The Cologne biologist Bruno Kremer established that the Rhine is 1,230 kilometres long. Owing to a wrong transcription in the 1960s, its length is always given as 1,320 kilometres.

● Afri-Cola, a drink derived from "African cola bean", comes from Cologne and was registered as a trademark on 26 June 1931 by F. Blumhoffer Nachfolger GmbH in the district Cologne-Braunsfeld.

● On 23 June 1963 John F. Kennedy shouted the Carnival call "Kölle alaaf" in front of Cologne's city hall.

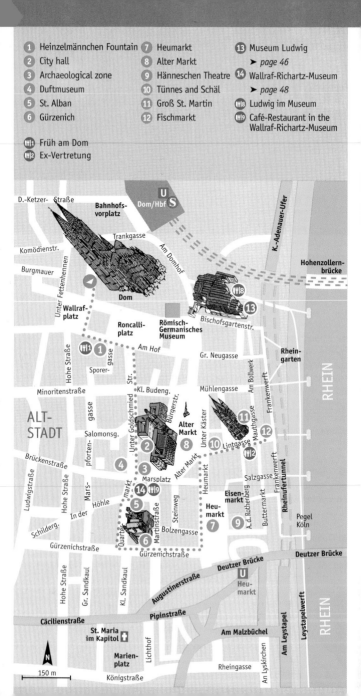

1. Heinzelmännchen Fountain
2. City hall
3. Archaeological zone
4. Duftmuseum
5. St. Alban
6. Gürzenich
7. Heumarkt
8. Alter Markt
9. Hänneschen Theatre
10. Tünnes and Schäl
11. Groß St. Martin
12. Fischmarkt
13. Museum Ludwig
    ➤ page 46
14. Wallraf-Richartz-Museum
    ➤ page 48

R1. Früh am Dom
R2. Ex-Vertretung
R18. Ludwig im Museum
R19. Café-Restaurant in the Wallraf-Richartz-Museum

Day 1

A Walk Around the City

Kölsche Lebensart
Cologne Art Gallery

A BUILDING SITE FOR 632 YEARS

It took more than six centuries to complete Cologne Cathedral. Around 70 years after the foundation stone was laid in 1248, the choir was consecrated,

but from then onwards construction work proceeded slowly and was officially halted in 1560 due to lack of money. For more than 300 years the massive torso with a builders' crane on the unfinished south tower was a landmark of the city. Work did not restart until 1842, now initiated by the Prussian authorities, and was completed on 15 October 1880.

COLOGNE CATHEDRAL – A WORLD HERITAGE SITE

How light is filtered through 11,263 coloured squares, why a shrine with holy relics has such precious decoration, and who are the patron saints of the city – find out in Cologne's most famous building.

These questions and many more can be answered by the gentlemen in red robes who carry wooden collection boxes. They are officially known as the cathedral *Swiss guard*, a reference to the pope's bodyguards, who traditionally come from Switzerland, and patiently answer every question. Their main duty is to maintain the proper atmosphere and good behaviour in the cathedral.

As if they were magnets, the two spires draw visitors to the cathedral, which rises like a dark giant between the rail tracks, busy roads and the overcrowded pedestrian zone. No other German city has an emblem like this. Planned to be the biggest cathedral in Europe, it is imposing for its huge dimensions alone: it covers an area of 8,000 square metres altogether, with a length of 144 metres and a width of 86 metres. The huge, colourful surfaces of window glass, a combined total of 10,000 square metres, are equally impressive.

It all began with an act of theft: after the conquest of Milan, in 1164

3 TIP Before your trip to Cologne, book a *tour above the roofs* of the city to see the elegant iron framework above the cathedral vaults, enjoy spectacular views and explore little-known tower chambers holding the stores and workshops of the cathedral builders. (Tel. 0221/17940555)

the bones of the Three Magi were brought to Cologne as spoils of war, making the city one of the most important places of pilgrimage in the Christian world.

On 15 August 1248 the foundation stone was laid for a new cathedral

in the latest style of the age, French Gothic. It was to act as a gigantic shrine for the relics and to surpass all existing buildings.

In order to house the relics, the goldsmith Nicolas of Verdun made the precious *shrine of the Three Magi*, dating from 1190–1220. It now stands behind the altar in the choir and is the main attraction inside the cathedral. Shaped like a basilica church, this is the largest reliquary shrine in the West. Its iconographic programme ranges from the Creation to the Last Judgement. The figures are fashioned from gilded copper, the front end of pure gold, complemented by filigree work in precious and semi-precious stones, including ancient gems and cameos.

The cathedral is also home to a host of important works of art. Among the most notable are the Gero Crucifix (made around the year 980), the oldest surviving monumental figure of the crucified Christ, and the *Altar of the City Patron Saints* by Stefan Lochner

CATHEDRAL BUILDERS

Cologne Cathedral was completed in 1880, but the building work has never stopped. Scaffolding can always be seen on the church, because preserving it is a job that never ends. The artisans of the cathedral office of works continue

a tradition of craftsmanship that has survived from the Middle Ages. Stonemasons and sculptors are responsible for renewing the weathered stonework. They are joined by roofers, scaffolders, carpenters, painters, electricians and metalworkers. Glass restorers, glass painters and glaziers take care of the conservation and restoration of the historic stained-glass windows. A goldsmith and a silversmith have the task of maintaining the works of precious metal in the treasury.

www.dombau-koeln.de

(around 1442), a masterpiece of the late Gothic Cologne school of painting in the Lady Chapel. A 21st-century work is the *window by the artist Gerhard Richter* in the south transept. Consisting of 11,263 squares of glass in 72 different shades of colour, when the sun shines it generates a symphony of light.

One sight should on no account be missed: to get a wonderful view of the city, climb the 533 steps of the south tower to the lookout deck at a height of 97 metres. On the way up you pass St Peter's bell, affectionately known to the people of Cologne as *Big Peter*, at 24 tonnes the biggest free-swinging church bell in the world.

Domkloster 4 ▲ Dom/Hbf.
◆ Cathedral: Mon-Sat 6am-7.30pm (Nov-Apr), 6am-9pm (May-Oct), Sun 1-4.30pm
◆ Treasury (Schatzkammer): 10am-6pm
◆ Tower: 9am-4pm (Nov-Feb), 9am-5pm (March, April, Oct), 9am-6pm (May-Sept)

www.domfuehrungen-koeln.de
www.koelner-dom.de
www.koelner-dommusik.de

Have a Break

Some time in a brewery pub (Brauhaus) is an essential part of a trip to Cologne. Enjoy a glass of Kölsch beer and the favourite snack, halve Hahn, (➤ p. 56) in **Früh am Dom**. *Am Hof 12-18*
◆ Mon-Fri 11am-midnight, Sat-Sun 9am-midnight
www.frueh-am-dom.de

The Old Town

ARCHAEOLOGICAL ZONE ③

In order to make the site of excavations of Roman, Jewish and medieval Cologne around the city hall accessible to the public, work is now being done on the Archaeological Zone, a subterranean museum covering an area of 8,500 square metres. On the open space in front of the city hall, a Jewish Museum will be built, protecting the remains of the synagogue and mikva, the Jewish ritual bath. At present only the Praetorium, with the walls and foundations of a monumental 4th-century palace, and a Roman sewer can be visited.

◆ *Tue-Sun 10am-5pm www.museenkoeln.de/ archaeologische-zone/*

THE OLD TOWN – ROMANS; ARCHBISHOPS AND CHARACTERS

Between the cathedral and the Rhine lies one of the most attractive quarters of the city. Shops, atmospheric eating places and traditional Brauhaus pubs are situated in little gabled houses, narrow alleys and picturesque squares.

● HEINZELMÄNNCHEN FOUNTAIN ①: Right next to Brauhaus Früh the best-loved fountain in the city shows how wonderful life might have been in Cologne. Stone reliefs tell the story of the busy elves who quietly, secretly came in the night to do all the unfinished work. They would have carried on their jobs if it had not been for an inquisitive tailor's wife, who wanted to uncover the secret. She scattered peas on the steps of her house. The elves slipped on them, fell down the steps and were discovered. Angry at this treatment, they left for ever, leaving the thankless citizens to do the work for themselves.

● CITY HALL ②: 2,000 years of city history are concentrated around the Rathaus (city hall). The oldest testimonies to this are the Praetorium, seat of the Roman governor, and the remains of the medieval Jewish quarter.

The imposing *tower of the city hall* and its magnificent *Renaissance loggia* (1569–73) bear witness to the wealth and pride of the burghers in past times. As early as 1130 they had a "house of the citizens", which is thought to be the oldest city hall in Germany.

The tower was built by the guilds of craftsman between 1407 and 1414 to demonstrate their rule of the city. With its five storeys, it is 61 metres tall and is decorated with a sculptural programme showing 130 characters from Cologne history, and the *Platzjabbek*, the wooden face of a figure wearing a broad-brimmed hat and a beard beneath the clock. When the clock strikes the hour, he opens his mouth and sticks out his tongue.

The showpiece inside the city hall is the long chamber on the upper floor, adorned with fine stone tracery. It is called the *Hansa Chamber* in memory of the conference of cities of the Hanseatic League that was held here in 1367. Stone statues of the *Nine Heroes* on the south wall symbolise good government; opposite them on the north wall are eight figures of prophets (c. 1410) taken from a nearby room.

Rathausplatz 2
Visits only as part of a guided tour:
tel. 0221/346430

THE GENUINE EAU DE COLOGNE

The history of eau de Cologne goes back over 300 years, before the time of the most famous brand, 4711. Johann Maria Farina created a fragrance called Farina Original Eau de Cologne and supplied it to royal courts and

rulers in the 18th century. His success was soon imitated: in 1803 Wilhelm Mülhens acquired rights to the name of a Mr Farina, who was not related to the perfumer, in order to advertise his own perfume as a Farina product, and even sold on the name rights to others. 80 years passed before the Farina family could register their name as the first-ever trademark in Germany. Then the Mülhens family renamed their perfume after their house number (➤ p. 34).

● PERFUME MUSEUM IN THE FARINA HOUSE ④: On the opposite corner of the city hall square stands the house where the story of eau de Cologne began. In his small perfumery opposite a little square, Gülichplatz, in 1709 the Italian Johann Maria Farina invented a fragrance that reminded him of an Italian spring morning after rain, with the scents of orange, lemon, grapefruit, bergamot and citron, the blossoms and herbs of his homeland. The perfume quickly became a sought-after product in the world of the rich and beautiful, who preferred using perfume to washing, a common practice in the Rococo era. To find out more about eau de Cologne and three centuries of perfume and social history, visit the perfume museum (Duftmuseum).

Obenmarspforten 21
♦ *Mon-Sat 10am-7pm, Sun 11am-5pm, visits only as part of a guided tour:*
tel. 0221/3998994
www.farina-haus.de

● **ST. ALBAN** ⑤: Right next to the Wallraf-Richartz-Museum are the ruins of St Alban's Church, today a place of memorial for the dead of the two world wars. In the bombed-out church stands a copy of Käthe Kollwitz's work *Grieving Parents* (1931), bearing the facial features of the artist and her husband in memory of their son, who fell in the First World War.

Quatermarkt 4

● **GÜRZENICH** ⑥: A little further on stands a major Gothic secular building. Constructed by the citizens of Cologne in the 15th century on land belonging to the patrician Gürzenich family, it served as a venue for celebrations and a storehouse. Today the Gürzenich is the city's best-known place for congresses and events. To reach the great hall on the first floor, once the scene of receptions for emperors and glittering festivities, visitors pass through the spacious foyer and curving staircase in the extension built in the 1950s.

Martinstrasse 29–31
Visits only as part of a guided tour:
tel. 0221/22123332

FOUNDERS OF THE CITY

Agrippa, who is portrayed on the ground floor of the Gürzenich, was a Roman general, a friend of Emperor Augustus. He was long thought to have founded Cologne, as he brought the Germanic Ubii tribe to the left bank of

the Rhine to be settled in the new town called Oppidum Ubiorum. In fact the credit for founding the city goes to Augustus, who order construction of an altar to the goddess Roma in 7 BC at which the Germanic tribes should pledge loyalty to the emperor each year, the basis for the community. The settlement gained its name Colonia Claudia Ara Agrippinensium (CCAA) in 50 AD, when Emperor Claudius, urged by his wife Agrippina, who was born there, granted municipal rights.

HÄNNESCHEN THEATRE ⑨

A shady courtyard is the home of the Hänneschen Theatre, a company with a long tradition that stages performances with puppets, a kind of commedia dell'arte in Kölsch, the Cologne dialect. The Hänneschen is a Cologne institution that has delighted children and adults since 1802 with puppets representing characters from the village of Knollendorf. Usually the

stories revolve around the everyday life of the main figures, Hänneschen and Bärbelchen. The characters Tünnes and Schäl are also involved, as is the fool of the ensemble, Speimanes, and the policeman Schnäutzerkowsky. All those who want to take a look behind the scenes can do so at the annual Hänneschen fair in May.

www.haenneschen.de

● **HEUMARKT** ⑦: Continue towards the Rhine to one of Cologne's largest squares. Heumarkt (Haymarket), an important place for trade in the Middle Ages, has been one of the leading open spaces of the city for centuries. It was once surrounded by the splendid gabled houses of merchants and artisans. As the approach to the bridge cut through it, it is now hard to imagine that this was once one of Europe's finest squares. The equestrian statue of King Friedrich Wilhelm III of Prussia, dating from 1878, surrounded by an illustrious circle of life-size figures including the Humboldt brothers, Friedrich Hegel, Ludwig van Beethoven, Karl Friedrich Schinkel and the art-collecting Boisserée brothers, commemorates the incorporation of the Rhineland into the state of Prussia.

● **ALTER MARKT** ⑧: A little further north lies Alter Markt, the commercial heart of medieval Cologne. The former appearance of this marketplace

can be seen by looking at the historic *Gaffelhaus* at Alter Markt no. 20/22. This Renaissance double building, the houses Zur Brezel and Zum Dorn, with their typical gables and fine windows, is one of the few imposing buildings that remain here.

The middle of the marketplace is occupied by the *Jan von Werth Fountain*, dedicated to a Cologne hero. Disappointed in love when he asked for the hand of the maid Griet, Jan von Werth hired as a soldier in the Thirty Years' War. Many years later, now a cavalry general, he entered his home town in triumph and, looking down from his horse, saw Griet, who had not married and was a poor market woman, selling apples by the city gate. When she recognised him, he said "Griet, if only you had married me!", at which she answered "Jan, if only I had known".

COLOGNE HUMOUR: THE KALLENDRESSER

Next to the Gaffelhaus, look up to see what Cologne people think of their rulers. Beneath the eaves there hangs a bronze figure called the Kallendresser ("one who shits in the gutter"), squatting and showing his naked backside to the city hall. According to a legend, the citizens were angry when the abbot of St Martin's handed over to the city authorities a criminal who had fled to the monastery hoping for sanctuary.

Alter Markt, the centre of the Old Town, is one of the pleasantest places in Cologne when the sun shines, and pubs, cafés and restaurants set up their tables and chairs outdoors.

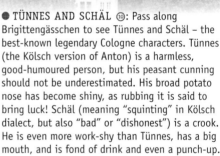

RIGHT OF STAPLE

In the Middle Ages Cologne was a prosperous place of trade. The wealth of the city increased even more in 1259 when Archbishop Konrad von Hochstaden awarded it the Right of Staple, an important privilege. From that time all ships were obliged to take their wares ashore and offer them for sale for three days. This law corresponded to a geographical factor: as the Middle Rhine is shallower than the Lower Rhine, the goods had anyway to be loaded onto a different kind of ship in Cologne.

● TÜNNES AND SCHÄL ⑩: Pass along Brigittengässchen to see Tünnes and Schäl – the best-known legendary Cologne characters. Tünnes (the Kölsch version of Anton) is a harmless, good-humoured person, but his peasant cunning should not be underestimated. His broad potato nose has become shiny, as rubbing it is said to bring luck! Schäl (meaning "squinting" in Kölsch dialect, but also "bad" or "dishonest") is a crook. He is even more work-shy than Tünnes, has a big mouth, and is fond of drink and even a punch-up. He has a love-hate relationship with Tünnes: neither of them can get along without the other.

● GROSS ST. MARTIN ⑪: Here stands the Romanesque church St Martin the Great (1150–1240) that, along with the cathedral, dominates the Rhine panorama thanks to its central tower and richly decorated choir with the ground-plan of a clover leaf. This basilica is both the emblem and the name-giving church of the St Martin's quarter. Inside, the imposing architecture and plain furnishing come as a surprise. Don't fail to descend into the crypt,

a journey back to Roman times. 2,000 years ago the site was an island, divided from the town by a channel of the Rhine, used first as a sports ground and later for building warehouses.

An Groß St. Martin
◆ *Tue-Sat 9am-7.30pm, Sun 1-7.15pm*
jerusalem.cef.fr/de/koeln-gross-sankt-martin

● FISCHMARKT ⑬:
The Fishmarket, with a colourful row of narrow houses crowned by gables, is one of the most attractive spots in the Old Town. In the Middle

Have a break

Ex-Vertretung is a pleasant place for watching the comings and goings on the riverside promenade. *Frankenwerft 31–33,* ◆ *11am-midnight, www.ex-vertretung.de*

Ages merchants dominated the scene in the little alleys round about. The tower of the old fish warehouse is a reminder of this at the corner of Mauthgasse. Until the Right of Staple was

abolished in 1831 it was used to store goods, and thus later got the name Stapelhaus.

FOLK MONUMENTS

In the Old Town local heroes and traditions are honoured. On Ostermannplatz a fountain refers to the songs of the Cologne singer Willi Ostermann (1876–1936). On Gülichplatz the bronze Fastnachtsbrunnen (1913) celebrates Carnival, and in the shadow of St Martin the Great a small open space called Rote-Funken-Plätzchen has a stone relief on the wall depicting a Carnival dancer (Funkenmariechen) with two members of a Carnival association and the text of the oath that they swear. An unusual monument is the square column (Schmitzsäule, 1969), 4.50 metres high, near Brigittengässchen, commemorating the "original" Rhinelander, whose typical name is Schmitz.

UGLY HEADS

In several places in the Old Town, grimacing stone heads can be seen on the walls (e.g. Salzgasse 2; Gasthaus zum St. Peter on Seidmacherinnengässchen). In the Middle Ages they had a practical purpose: instead of a lower jaw there was a hole in the wall into which a post was pushed. A rope thrown over the post was used to lower barrels or sacks into the cellar.

● STREET NAMES THAT TELL OF HISTORY: On a walk through the Old Town you will see many unusual street names that tell of the history of this district. *Obenmarspforten* (Upper Mars Gate) refers to the time when the Roman harbour was built and the Mars Gate near this street was an entrance to the city from the river bank. *Judengasse* (Jews' Alley) and *Salomongasse* go back to the Middle Ages, when part of the Old Town was the Jewish quarter. The painters of signs (Schilder) lived in *Schildergasse*, the goldsmiths and silversmiths in the street *Unter Goldschmied*. Butter was bought and sold on *Buttermarkt*, fish was stored in the fish warehouse on *Fischmarkt*, and preserved in salt, for which the traders lived in *Salzgasse*. In *Lintgasse*, the basket makers used bast (Lint) to make ropes and baskets for fish. Around the corner in *Unter Käster* the barrels for Cologne's most famous export items, salted herring, were produced. The merchants sold their wares at stalls (Buden), which gave the streets *Kleine Budengasse* and *Grosse Budengasse* their names. Textiles were important items for Cologne's industry, as shown by the streets *Kämmergasse* (Combers' Alley), *Filzengraben* (Felt Moat) and *Rothgerberbach* (Red Tanners' Stream). Blue dye was made from the plant woad (Waid), which regional farmers sold in Cologne at *Waidmarkt* to the blue dyers, who lived and worked on *Blaubach*.

Lintgasse

Cologne in the Evening

The Old Town

Cathedral

Art Museums

Along the Rhine

Cologne in the Evening

Romanesque Churches

Shopping and Strolling

3 Days in

COLOGNE CARNIVAL

On the Thursday before Lent, when Fastelovend (Carnival) is opened on Alter Markt at 11.11 am, public life in Cologne comes to a stop. Everyone shouts "Kölle Alaaf" (Up with Cologne!), and revellers sing and dance everywhere, in the streets and in the pubs. The

top event is the parade on Carnival Monday (Rosenmontag). More than a million spectators line the route and hope to catch the sweets and flowers that are thrown from the floats. At the burning of Nubbel, a straw-stuffed doll, at midnight on the Tuesday, they say farewell to Carnival with tears in their eyes and yearn for the start of the new season on 11 November.

COLOGNE IN THE EVENING – FROM CLUBBING TO CLASSICAL OPERA

In Cologne there is so much to do in the evening that it is hard to choose. From theatre and concerts to a multicultural festival or a DJ night, in the Old Town or the Belgian Quarter, there are many options for entertainment!

● CULTURE: Cologne has a widely varied cultural life. In the Philharmonie, one of Europe's most beautiful and best concert halls, a high-class programme is staged. Concerts of ancient or modern music, including journeys to musical cultures around the world, can be heard at the *Musikhochschule* and the *Funkhaus* of broadcaster WDR. Cologne is known for its lively and innovative jazz scene: in the *Stadtgarten, Altes Pfandhaus, Loft* and many other jazz venues, everything from classic big-band music to experimental jazz is on offer.

The *E-Werk, Alter Wartesaal* and *MTC* are just a few of the locations where everything from Kölschrock to hiphop and house is played. And with the *LANXESS arena*, Cologne has the biggest indoor hall in Germany – not to forget the opera ensemble, which is performing in the Staatenhaus on the right bank of the Rhine until the refurbishment of the opera house has been completed. Cologne's theatre scene is equally diverse. In addition to the municipal companies, for example the Schauspiel playing on the Carlswerk site in the Mülheim district (➤ p. 61) and the *Hänneschen Theatre* (➤ p. 18), countless independent theatre ensembles enrich the cultural life of the city. Whether you like political satire or experimental drama, stand-up comedy or farce, there is something for every taste. To see listings of the programme of independent theatres, go to *www.theaterszene-koeln.de*. If you prefer literature, take a look at the programme of the *Literaturhaus Köln*.

● GOING OUT: One of the best-known areas is the Altstadt (Old Town), where numerous pubs and clubs attract tourists and visitors from outside the city. The younger age groups go more often to the Ring, where they can party until the early hours at *Nachtflug, Diamonds Club, Das Ding, Ivory* and *Vanity*.

BAP

"Verdamp lang her" (a hell of a long time ago) is the name of their best-known song, and it is indeed a long time since the band BAP was founded. In 1976 the singer and songwriter Wolfgang Niedecken, the "Bob Dylan of the Südstadt", started his Kölschrock band with other musicians. With role models like Bob Dylan, the Rolling Stones and Bruce Springsteen, today BAP is one of the most successful rock bands in the German-speaking

world, now going for 40 years. Its membership has changed several times, but old songs such as "Kristallnaach", "Verdamp lang her" and "Aff un zo" still enthuse the public. BAP can fill Germany's biggest concert halls, but they have never lost their love of Cologne, and to all the songs expressing that love they have added their own: "Dausende vun Liebesleeder".

www.bap.de

The party continues in the **Friesenviertel** around Friesenstrasse in *Päffgen*, with Cologne's oldest in-house brewery, *Jameson's Irish Pub*, trendy places like *Heising & Adelmann* and *Päff*, and cult pubs such as *Klein-Köln*. Try *Hemingway* for cocktails, *Goldfinger* for dancing.

Cologne's student quarter and probably its biggest party zone is the **Kwartier Latäng** (Latin Quarter) around Zülpicher Strasse. Old-established pubs like *Oma Kleinmann* and cult locations like *Stiefel*, the brew-pub *Hellers Brauhaus* and *Roonburg* are popular locations here.

The hip area is the **Belgisches Viertel** (Belgian Quarter, ➤ p. 36), where a host of small cafés, bars and restaurants have sprung up between designer shops and galleries. The heart of the scene is St Michael's Church on Brüsseler Platz, an open-air rendezvous in Cologne in summer. *Café Bauturm* and *Café Schmitz* on Aachener Strasse are Cologne institutions. *Ouzeria* and *Belgischer Hof* are just two of the attractive little restaurants around here.

Cologne people love their own Veedel (quarter).

One of the most popular is the **Südstadt**, with its concentration of pubs. The attraction here is the mix of authentic Cologne style of *Früh im Veedel*, long-established trendy joints like *Opera* and *Filos*, and newer clubs such as *Tsunami*.

Alternative subculture is found in **Ehrenfeld**, with a party scene in the *Live Music Hall*, the *Art Theater* and *Club Bahnhof Ehrenfeld*. The many pubs and bars include *Meer sehen*, *Hängende Gärten* and *Königsblut*.

There is plenty going on across the Rhine (➤ p. 44): dancing to techno in *Bootshaus* in **Mülheim Harbour** and in *Elektroküche* at the Essigfabrik in Deutz. On the Rhine in **Deutz** there is no nicer place in good weather than *km 689 – Cologne Beach Club*. For traditional Kölsch style, go to the *Brauhaus ohne Namen* and *Lommerzheim,* a pub with cult status.

For listings on where to go out in Cologne, see *koelnparty.de*.

Romanesque Churches

The Old Town · Cathedral · Art Museums · Along the Rhine · Shopping and Strolling · Romanesque Churches · Cologne in the Evening

3 Days in

THE LEGEND OF ST URSULA

The legend says that Ursula, a Breton princess on a pilgrimage with ten girl companions and her bridegroom Aetherius, came from Rome to Cologne, where they fell into the hands of the Huns and were killed. At this a host of angels drove the heathen Huns from the gates of the city. In gratitude for their deliverance, the people of Cologne buried the holy virgins and dedicated a church to them. To this day the eleven flames in the city coat of arms refer to the martyrdom.

ROMANESQUE CHURCHES – STORIES OF SAINTS

In a city where there was once a church for every day of the year, including a collection of Romanesque churches unique in the world, a visit to at least one of them is a must. If that is not enough, there is the unusual museum of the archdiocese of Cologne, where modern and ancient religious art are shown side by side.

● ST URSULA ①: Have you ever been in a "chamber of horrors"? If not, don't fail to visit the church dedicated to Cologne's patron saint, Ursula. A Baroque tower roof with a golden crown shows the way to this Romanesque basilica, consecrated in 1135. On the galleries above the aisles were displayed bones that were thought to be holy relics from the martyrdom of St Ursula and her followers, discovered in the Middle Ages on the site of a Roman cemetery. As a huge number of bones were found, in popular belief the number of holy virgins was inflated from 11 to 11,000, attracting many pilgrims to the city.

Countless bones, artistically arranged to depict symbols and inscriptions, and over 100 reliquaries in gilded niches adorn the walls of the 17th-century Golden Chamber, generally known as the Schreckenskammer (chamber of horrors). This is only one part of the church's fine interior furnishings, which include 24 painted panels of the St Ursula cycle by Jan van Scheyven (1456) about the life of Cologne's patron saint.

Ursulaplatz 24 (Nordstadt)
tel. 0221/7880750
▲ *Breslauer Platz*
◆ *Mon-Sat 10am-12 noon, 3-5pm, Sun 3-5pm*
gemeinden.erzbistum-koeln.de/st_ursula_koeln/

HOLY COLOGNE

Cologne was a prosperous city in the Middle Ages, and its wealth of buildings is testimony to this. Before the mid-12th century it was the first German city to have its own city hall. Between 1150 and 1250, Cologne was like one huge building site: streets and squares were paved, a new city wall and 100 or more fine private residences were erected, and construction work took place on 28 churches, almost all at the same time. The citizens of Cologne thus earned for their city the proud title "Sancta Colonia", its title from the 12th century onwards.

● **ST ANDREAS** ②: The interaction of medieval and contemporary art in a church can be seen in the late Romanesque Dominican church of St Andreas, where the crypt holds the tomb of a sainted doctor of the church, Albertus Magnus. The architecture is a fine combination of the Romanesque and Gothic styles, contrasting the opulent, ornamental sculptural elements of the Romanesque nave with the simple elegance of the late Gothic choir.

RELICS FEVER

No German city in the Middle Ages had as many magnificent churches as Cologne. One reason for the construction boom was the veneration of holy relics. As these

relics – the remains of saints – were thought to have supernatural powers and could work miracles, the churches were filled with more and more of these treasures, displayed in precious receptacles and golden shrines. The numbers of pilgrims who flocked to the relics led to the rebuilding of churches – for example in 1106, when the graves of Ursula and her followers were thought to have been found, and after the entrance of the bones of the Three Magi into the city in 1164.

No less impressive is the modern stained glass by the artist Marcus Lüpertz, which draws the eye like a "gateway to heaven". In the north transept, where Gothic murals depict scenes from the life of the Virgin Mary, the windows are devoted to the teachings of Albertus Magnus. In the south transept, known as the Maccabee choir because a golden shrine containing relics of the Maccabees decorated with episodes from the legend of the Maccabee brothers is placed there, the windows are also devoted to their martyrdom.

Komödienstrasse 6–8 (city centre)
tel. 0221/160660
▲ *Dom/Hbf.*
◆ *Mon 7.30am-6pm, Sat-Sun 8am-6pm*
www.sankt-andreas.de

● ST GEREON ③: The remarkable interior of a third Romanesque church, dedicated to St Gereon, is a good reason to add this one, too, to the list of visits. According-ing to a medieval legend, Gereon was a Roman military officer who died for his Christian faith along with 318 legionary soldiers. When you enter the ten-sided building with its massive dome, slender pillars draw the gaze upwards. The glowing red of the dome with golden flames that refer to the Holy Spirit at Pentecost and the modern windows by

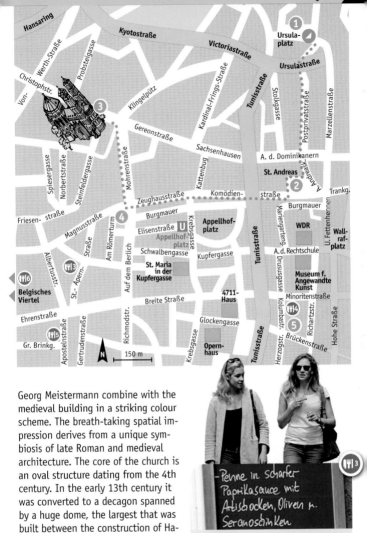

Georg Meistermann combine with the medieval building in a striking colour scheme. The breath-taking spatial impression derives from a unique symbiosis of late Roman and medieval architecture. The core of the church is an oval structure dating from the 4th century. In the early 13th century it was converted to a decagon spanned by a huge dome, the largest that was built between the construction of Hagia Sophia in Constantinople in the 6th century and the dome of Florence cathedral in the 15th century.

Gereonsdriesch 2–4
tel. 0221/4745070
▲ *Christophstrasse*
◆ *Mon-Sat 10am-6pm, Sun 1-6pm*
www.stgereon.de

Have a break

After all this church architecture, take refreshments at the **Hase** restaurant with its Mediterranean cuisine and bistro atmosphere.
St.-Apern-Strasse 17
◆ *Mon-Sat 12 noon-4pm, 6pm-1am*
www.hase-restaurant.de

● KOLUMBA (ART MUSEUM OF THE ARCHDIOCESE) ⑤:
The value of preserving memories and an example of responsible treatment of historic heritage is shown by the art museum of the archdiocese. The austere yet refined new building designed by the Swiss architect Peter Zumthor combines an archaeological excavation with the ruins of the late Gothic St Kolumba Church and the chapel Madonna in den Trümmern (Madonna of the Ruins) by Gottfried Böhm to form a harmonious trinity of place, collection and architecture.

ROMAN TOWER ④

That Roman architecture can survive the passage of time is shown by the north-western corner tower of the Roman city

wall, at the junction of St.-Apern-Strasse with Zeughausstrasse. Used in the Middle Ages as a latrine by the neighbouring convent of Poor Clares, and in the 19th century as the lower floor of a house, it is very well preserved. Mosaic patterns of various kinds of stone adorn the façade; the cornice and crenellations were added in around 1900.

Inside it is a lively museum with a "permanently moving inventory". Selected works from a remarkable collection that ranges from the early Christian period to contemporary art are presented according to changing themes, and visitors are invited to open up to unaccustomed sensory impressions. The museum team has long experience at creating contrasts between medieval saints' figures, madonnas and monstrances with works by August Macke, Andy Warhol or Joseph Beuys.

Kolumbastrasse 4,
tel. 0221/9331930
▲ *Dom/Hbf.* ◆ *Wed-Mon 12 noon-5pm*
www.kolumba.de

Have a break

You have surely earned a stop to drink coffee. On your way is **Espresso Perfetto**.
Kolumbastrasse 8 ◆ *Mon-Sat 8am-7pm*
www.espressoperfetto.de

Shopping and Strolling

The Old Town

Cologne in the Evening

Cathedral

Art Museums

3 Days in

Romanesque Churches

Along the Rhine

Shopping and Strolling

STROLLING AND SHOPPING – AROUND NEUMARKT

COLOGNE'S BEST-KNOWN HOUSE NUMBER: 4711

Every hour, on the hour, a glockenspiel rings out on the neo-Gothic façade of a house in Glockengasse that has Cologne's best-known house number: 4711. This is the brand name of a famous eau de Cologne, and recalls the years of French

For exclusive fashion around Mittelstrasse or hip shops in Ehrenstrasse, for branches of famous retail chains in Schildergasse and Hohe Strasse or young designers in the Belgian Quarter – in the centre of Cologne you can go on an endless shopping tour.

In the pedestrian zone along two main streets, *Schildergasse* and *Hohe Strasse*, which connect Neumarkt with the central station, fashion outlets and department stores as well as branches of international chains present their wares for window shopping. Crowds of shoppers come here from morning to evening and all year round. An eye-catching building here is the Weltstadthaus by the star architect Renzo Piano. It has a resemblance to a glass whale, and is used by Peek & Cloppenburg to present an enormous clothing assortment on four floors *(Schildergasse 65–67)*.

occupation. The French numbered all the buildings in the city consecutively, and the address of the Mülhens company (sold in 1994 to the Wella group) was given the number 4711.

Have a break

For breakfast or a snack, but ideally for its outstandingly fine patisserie goods, the café **Törtchen Törtchen** is seventh heaven for everyone with a sweet tooth.
Apostelnstrasse 19 ◆ Mon-Sat 9am-7pm, Sun 10am-6pm, www.toertchentoertchen.de

A well-loved attraction, not only for children, is the Lego Store on Hohe Strasse, where you can play with the coloured bricks to your heart's delight *(Hohe Strasse 68)*.

For exquisite and unusual items, or simply to do some window shopping, Mittelstrasse and Pfeilstrasse to the west of Neumarkt are an excellent destination. In the most expensive shopping street in Cologne and its side streets, exclusive fashion boutiques alternate with shops selling other extravagant goods. To cast your eye over international luxury labels, pass through the bright pink tunnel that leads to the Apropos Concept-Store *(Mittelstrasse 12)*.

Via *Apostelnstrasse*, where the old-established Filz Gnoss (felt goods; no. 21) is still in business, go on to Ehrenstrasse. Here stores for coveted labels have appeared between shops specialising in hip and in-your-face fashion. The esoterically inclined, shoe fetishists and lovers of kitsch will all find something to please. This street is a place to see and be seen, especially for a young crowd. If you prefer art and antiques, then nearby *St.-Apern-Strasse* around the Kreishausgalerie is the place to browse in galleries and antique shops.

KONRAD ADENAUER

On the north side of St. Aposteln Church stands a monument to Konrad Adenauer (1876–1967), mayor of Cologne and first chancellor of the Federal Republic. He was famous for his idiosyncratic ways of getting things done. While he was mayor (1917–33) the university was refounded, the trade fair grounds, Mülheim Bridge and Cologne-Bonn highway were built, the inner and outer green belts established and the Ford motor factory opened. "You achieve success in politics by being able to stay on your seat longer than the others," said Adenauer, a freeman of the city of Cologne.

3 **TIP** Twice a year, in the hip Belgian Quarter, the **Tour Belgique** opens almost every door and Brüsseler Platz turns into one huge catwalk and an open-air arena. The district devotes itself to culture, music, shopping and clubbing, shops stay open until 10pm and put on a special programme ranging from readings to concerts. Live music, live acts and other performances take over the bars, while cool after-show parties are held in the clubs. Artists present their work and the quarter becomes a single, big open-air gallery (www.le-tourbelgique.de). At the **le bloc festival** the Belgian Quarter shows what it has to offer in the field of fashion (www.lebloc.de).

THE RING – ONCE THE PLACE TO PROMENADE

In the late 19th century the Ring, which forms a semi-circle around the city, was one of Cologne's most popular shopping streets. In the age of industrialisation the city was bursting at the seams, until in 1881 the medieval city walls were torn down and, following the example of Paris and Vienna, a broad boulevard with trees, fountains and monuments was laid out. Today only the renovated stretch on Kaiser-Wilhelm-Ring serves as a reminder of those days.

To leave the mainstream, go to the Belgisches Viertel (Belgian Quarter) around St Michael's Church. Young fashion and jewellery designers have set up shop in attractive old buildings. Visitors will find little-known brands, vinyl records, books, paper goods, gifts and much more.

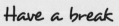

Have a break

With a view out onto Brüsseler Platz, stop at **Hallmackenreuther** to watch the goings-on and recover from shopping in a 1950s ambience.
Brüsseler Platz 9 ◆ *11am-1am*
www.hallmackenreuther.de

Day 3

Along the Rhine

The Old Town

Cathedral

Cologne in the Evening

Art Museums

3 Days in

Romanesque Churches

Along the Rhine

Shopping and Strolling

HOHENZOLLERN BRIDGE

If you climb the cathedral tower, you can see that the Hohenzollernbrücke (1907–11) is in line with the axis of the cathedral. The previous bridge, the first permanent Rhine bridge in Cologne since Roman times, was built in the mid-19th century

with the same alignment. It was the wish of King Friedrich Wilhelm IV of Prussia that the railway bridge, as a symbol of technical progress, and the cathedral, an important medieval building and symbol of the German nation, should relate to one another.

ALONG THE RHINE – BRIDGES, BOATS AND A MUSEUM FULL OF CHOCOLATE

This walk starts from Heumarkt and passes Romanesque architecture and painting in Cologne's newest district, the redeveloped harbour called Rheinauhafen, and from there crosses the river.

● ST MARIA IM KAPITOL ①: From Heumarkt it is well worthwhile making a small detour to one of the oldest and largest Romanesque churches in Cologne (1065), which occupies the site of the Roman Capitoline temple. The magnificent combination of the nave with a "clover-leaf" choir, the first in the Rhineland, modelled on the Church of the Nativity in Bethlehem, was to point the way ahead for Romanesque architecture on the Rhine. Inside the church is a real gem: 11th-century carved wooden doors, with some traces of their original colours, that tell the story of the life and Passion of Christ. One curiosity inside is a so-called rib of the Virgin Mary, in fact a bone from the ribcage or jaws of a Greenland whale that had found its way into an arm of the Rhine in the Pleistocene era. Outside on Marienplatz is the Gate of the Three Kings, through which the relics of the Three Magi were brought on their procession into the city in 1164.

Marienplatz 19
◆ *Mon-Sat 9am-6pm, Sun 11.30am-5pm*
www.maria-im-kapitol.de

● OVER-
STOLZEN-
HAUS ②: In
Rheingasse
stands a Roman-
esque house,
the only one
that remains of
the impressive
patrician family resi-
dences from that peri-
od. Today it is occupied
by the Kunsthochschule
für Medien (Academy of
Media Arts). The opulent
adornment of its five-bay
façade with four storeys in its
stepped gable, used for storage,
testify to the wish of the Over-
stolz family to display the wealth
they earned in the wine trade. They
built the house in about 1220/30 as
a place to live and do business.

Rheingasse 8 ◆ Mon-Thu 10am-6pm,
Fri 10am-3pm, www.khm.de

● ST MARIA
LYSKIRCHEN ③:
On the way to the
river you pass a small
church that is closely associated with the Rhine. It
was built in about 1210/20
right behind the city wall in
a suburb populated by fisher-
men and river boatmen. Until
1868 the late Gothic "Boatmen's
Madonna" that is now in the north
aisle stood in a niche in the outer
walls to bless passing boats. Inside
the church, the colourful murals and ceiling paintings of the
13th century have survived the passage of time with little dam-
age, and several restorations.

An Lyskirchen 12 ◆ 9am-6pm
www.lyskirchen.com

UP AND DOWN THE RHINE BY BOAT

What would Cologne be without the Rhine (apart from having a cathedral)? The city is seen at its best from the river, and therefore a boat trip is an essential part of any visit to Cologne. For a brunch or a dinner with music and dancing, or simply for a cruise with a view, a round trip takes about an hour, passing the Old Town and going south to the old fishing village of Rodenkirchen or upriver past the Rhine cable car and the zoo to Mülheim and back.

Trips start from several piers between the bridges Hohenzollernbrücke and Deutzer Brücke:

KD Köln-Düsseldorfer Deutsche Rheinschiff- fahrt AG tel. 0221/2088318 www.k-d.com

Dampfschifffahrt Colonia tel. 0221/2574225 www.dampfschiffahrt- colonia.de

KölnTourist Personenschiff- fahrt am Dom GmbH tel. 0221/121600 www.koelntourist.net

● RHEINAUHAFEN: Cross a hydraulic swing-bridge next to the so-called Malakoff Tower, part of the Prussian city defences, to see the newest highlight of modern urban planning in Cologne, the Rheinauhafen harbour area. Built over 100 years ago for the trade in grain and wood, it has now become an attractive district for living, work-ing and culture, with a fascinating juxtaposition of late 19th-century and modern architecture. On all sides you see the combination of historic materials such as stone paving, train rails and re-stored harbour cranes with huge slabs of concrete, steel and glass, set off by high-class lighting design. Despite the renewal of its appearance, the Rheinauhafen has not lost its original harbour character.

● CHOCOLATE MUSEUM ☺: The eye-catching building be-yond the swing-bridge, a glass palace that looks like the bows of a ship, was skil-fully and harmoniously blended with the old customs offices. In 1993 Hans Imhoff, owner of the Stollwerck chocolate

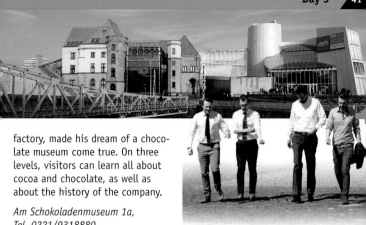

factory, made his dream of a chocolate museum come true. On three levels, visitors can learn all about cocoa and chocolate, as well as about the history of the company.

Am Schokoladenmuseum 1a,
Tel. 0221/9318880
◆ *Tue-Fri 10am-6pm,*
Sat-Sun 11am-7pm
www.schokoladenmuseum.de

● GERMAN SPORTS AND OLYMPIC MUSEUM ⑨: If you don't have a weakness for the sweet world of chocolate, walk a few steps further to the Deutsches Sport- und Olympiamuseum, housed in a protected monument, the old customs warehouse no. 10. On some 2,000 square metres of exhibition and event space it illuminates many different aspects of national, international and Olympic sports history, from ancient times to the present. The subject of trendy sports has its own room.

Im Zollhafen 1, tel. 0221/336090
◆ *Tue-Fri 9am-6pm, Sat-Sun 11am-7pm*
www.sportmuseum-koeln.de

---

3 TIP For a stunning bird's-eye view of Cologne, take a trip in the cable car that crosses the Rhine at a height of 50 metres.

▲ Zoo/Flora and Rheinpark
◆ reopening in 2019
www.koelner-seilbahn.de

SEVERIN'S QUARTER

Between Chlodwigplatz and the bridge Severinsbrücke lies a quarter with an authentic, typically Cologne character, where natives of the city and newcomers, some of them foreigners, live side by side. Cologne people love this area for its Mediterranean atmosphere. In the narrow streets with little old houses there are many attractive shops, pubs, cafés and restaurants. Officially this district is Altstadt-Süd (Old Town South), but in dialect it is called the Vringsveedel. "Vrings" is the local version of the name of Bishop Severin. The church dedicated to this saint is one of the oldest in Cologne, and a landmark in the quarter.

Near the sports museum you can admire a well-planned combination of protected historic buildings with modern architecture: next to old warehouses on the peninsula between the harbour basin and Rhine, the three tall "*crane buildings*" ⑥ by Hadi Teherani are among the architectural highlights. The striking shape of these glass high-rises is a reminder of the cargo cranes of the old port. They are now a significant feature on the city skyline. Passing the *Rhine bastion* ⑦ and the *Kontorgebäude* ⑧, once an office building, walk on to an emblem of the city, a row of historic warehouses called the *Siebengebirge* (Seven Peaks) ⑨ because of their conspicuous gables. Now they house luxury apartments. Beyond them lies the modern *Kap am Südkai* ⑩, a ten-storey structure with a roof garden at the south end of the harbour development.

A major monument of the city is the *Bayenturm* ⑪, a fortified medieval tower – now seat of a feminist research foundation, the Frauen-MediaTurm – that was stormed in 1262 by the people of Cologne, protesting against the rule of the archbishop. A popular saying has always maintained that whoever holds the tower holds power in the city. The next eye-catcher is the neo-Romanesque red-brick *harbour office* with its square clock tower, today the headquarters of the Cologne harbour and freight company, HGK.

ART COLOGNE

For a week each year, Cologne becomes a focus of the international art market. For the Art Cologne trade fair in spring, visitors from all around the world come to the displays of over 250 exhibiting galleries from Germany and abroad. It started in 1967 when a few gallery owners, including Hein Stünke and Rudolf Zwirner, founded the Kölner Kunstmarkt (Cologne Art Market) and showed contemporary work by little-known artists in the Gürzenich. The success of Art Cologne, as it has been called since 1984, was so huge that further art fairs have been established since then. The event Art.Fair in late autumn, originally an small appendage to Art Cologne, is now one of the three biggest art fairs, presenting international 21st-century art.

Continue on the landward side of the leisure marina to *Kunsthaus Rhenania* ⑫. In this con-

verted warehouse, 50 artists from various countries work together on interdisciplinary projects. Unconventional architecture is on view at the *RheinauArtOffice* ⑬, occupied by Microsoft: two parallel façade strips link its separate parts and frame the transparent glass front. These self-supporting strips make intermediate walls unnecessary. Art is the theme once again in the *art'otel* ⑭ at the end of the marina, which is adorned with works by the young Korean artist SEO, a pupil of Georg Baselitz.

www.artcologne.de
www.art-fair.de

Have a break

For mezedes and other Mediterranean delicacies, stop at **Limani** – the Greek word for harbour – in the Rheinkontor building.
Agrippinawerft 6 ◆ noon-0.30am, www.limanicologne.de

THE WRONG SIDE

Regarded by the Romans as barbarian, by archbishops as the land of heathen and by Mayor Adenauer as the first outpost of Siberia, the right bank of the Rhine has always had to bear prejudices. Its dialect name, "Schäl Sick", meaning literally "the squinty side", comes from the horses that pulled ships upstream and wore blinkers over their eyes to shield them from the sun. This made them squint, and they could not see the right bank of the river.

● RHEINBOULEVARD: Walk across the Deutzer Brücke to the other side of the Rhine, where the new Rhine boulevard including a flight of steps 500 metres long in front of the Hyatt Hotel is a good spot to linger a while. From here you have a superb panoramic view of the Old Town and the cathedral. It is one of the best places in Cologne to watch the sun go down.

● DEUTZ: For a long time the district of Deutz, which originated in a Roman fort, was overshadowed by the city quarters on the left bank of the Rhine. In the meantime Deutz has become a trendy quarter with a strong economic base thanks to the trade fair Koelnmesse, LANXESS arena, the TV company RTL, Lufthansa, Talanx/Gerling insurance, bee line and the Designpost. The most conspicuous landmark on the right bank is the innovative office high-rise called KölnTriangle. But this is also a good area to live, with a lot of pubs and restaurants. Thanks to the events at the Tanzbrunnen and in the LANXESS arena, Deutz buzzes with life, and both the Rhine promenade and Rhineside park are popular with walkers, joggers and tourists.

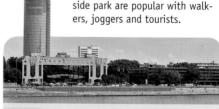

3 **TIP** For a magnificent view of the cathedral and surrounding area, take a lift 100 metres up to the viewing deck of the **KölnTriangle**. *Ottoplatz 1 ◆ Mon-Fri 12 noon-8pm, Sat-Sun 10am-8pm (Oct-Apr), Mon-Fri 11am-11pm, Sat-Sun 10am-11pm (May-Sept) www.koelntriangle.de*

Art Museums

PATRONS OF ART

When the Museum Ludwig reopened in late 2001 with an exhibition entitled "Museum of Our Wishes", this was a celebration of a fine tradition of collecting and donating. Ever since the 19th century, citizens of Cologne have played an active part in shaping the municipal collections. When the French occupying government dissolved the monasteries and

religious foundations in 1802–03, Ferdinand Franz Wallraf and the Boisserée brothers bought works of art and libraries. The great patrons of the 20th century included Alexander Schnütgen, Josef Haubrich, Adele Rautenstrauch and Wilhelm Joest, Hans Imhoff and Peter and Irene Ludwig.

ART MUSEUMS – A PASSION FOR COLLECTING

Whether you would like to see the most important currents and viewpoints in modern art or follow the development of painting in Cologne between 1300 and 1550 – in this art city on the Rhine, both are possible.

● MUSEUM LUDWIG: Just as the museum catches the eye from outside with its stepped architectural landscape of brick-red walls and curved roofs, inside it holds an exceptional collection that delights art lovers. Since being rearranged, the presentation is chronological, and will be in a state of constant change so that visitors can see, little by little, as broad a selection from the holdings as possible.

A circuit begins on the second floor with **modern works** that Josef Haubrich left to the city in his legacy of 1946. With works by Otto Dix,

Emil Nolde and Marc Chagall, Ernst Ludwig Kirchner's *Semi-Nude with a Hat* and Max Pechstein's *Fränzi on the Sofa*, paintings by Max Beckmann from the collection of Lilly von Schnitzler and much more, this is one of the leading collections of Expressionist art. The **Picasso collection**, the third-biggest in the world after those in Paris and Barcelona, is no less spectacular thanks to donations by Peter and Irene Ludwig. From *Harlequin* (1923) to *Woman with an Artichoke* (1941), all phases of the artist's work are represented, with paintings, ceramic works and sculptures. Russian avant-garde, Surrealist and Constructivist works round off the displays.

The exhibition on the first floor ranges from the abstract movement of the 1950s to the 1970s, including Action Painting, Minimal Art and Fluxus. Its highlight is the high-calibre **collection of Pop Art**, containing famous works such as Roy Lichtenstein's *Blonde M-Maybe – A Girl's Picture* (1965), Andy Warhol's *White Brillo Boxes* and Claes Oldenburg's *Soft Washstand*. Duane Hanson's famous *Woman with a Purse*, which puzzles visitors because it looks so real, is also here.

Have a break

After so much art you deserve a glass of Prosecco in the café **Ludwig im Museum**!
Heinrich-Böll-Platz (in the Museum Ludwig) ◆ *Tue-Sun 10am-midnight*

The stairs to the lower floor lead straight to A. R. Penck's monumental painting *I in Germany (West)* (1984) and thus to **contemporary art**. Two installations, *Heaven's Book* by the Chinese artist Xu Bing and *Regatta* by the Cuban Kcho, represent Asian and Latin American works here for the first time.

It is certainly worth viewing the *Photographic Collection*, one of the most significant in the world. It includes early daguerreotypes, rare early works of photography from the 19th century, important artistic photographs, albums and extensive material on the cultural history of this medium.

*Heinrich-Böll-Platz
tel. 0221/22126165
▲ Dom/Hbf.
◆ Tue-Sun 10am-6pm,
first Thu in the month
10am-10pm
www.museum-ludwig.de*

● WALLRAF-RICHARTZ-MUSEUM & FONDATION CORBOUD: The Cologne architect Oswald M. Ungers designed the austerely cuboid structure that harmoniously blends with the historic buildings of the neighbourhood thanks to its simple geometrical form. Visitors are guided through various eras of art history on three floors and can see paintings made over seven centuries, from medieval beginnings until the early 20th century.

Two angels hold open a precious brocade curtain, revealing the Virgin Mary in paradise, surrounded by more angels making music. Stefan Lochner's painting for private meditation, *Madonna in the Rose Garden* (c. 1450) – also known as the "Kölsch Mona Lisa" – is just one of many masterpieces in the gallery with the world's most comprehensive **collection of medieval painting** on the first floor.

Jusepe de Ribera's *Paulus Eremita* (1647), Rembrandt's famous *Self-Portrait* (c. 1668) and François Boucher's *Girl in Repose* (1751) can be mentioned as examples of the Baroque art on the floor above. The art

of the 17th and 18th centuries is represented through works by famous artists including Rubens, Bordone and Tintoretto, Murillo and Ribera.

A walk around the third floor takes the visitor from landscape painting of the early 19th century to the dawn of modern art. Impressionism is a strong point of the collection: with Auguste Renoir's *A Couple* (c. 1868), Vincent van Gogh's *Drawbridge* (1888) and Claude Monet's *Waterlilies* (1915/17), thanks to the collection of the Fondation Corboud art lovers can follow the course of Impressionism from its roots in Barbizon to the cube forms of Paul Cézanne and the Pointillist masterpieces of Paul Signac.

Tel. 0221/22121119
▲ *Dom/Hbf.*
◆ *Tue-Sun 10am-6pm, first and third Thu in the month 10am-10pm*
www.wallraf.museum

Have a break

Round off your visit to the museum with coffee and cake in the Wallraf-Richartz café-restaurant in the museum. *Café-Restaurant im Museum ◆ Tue-Sun 10am-6pm, first and third Thu 10am-10pm*

Accommodation, entertainment, tips and addresses

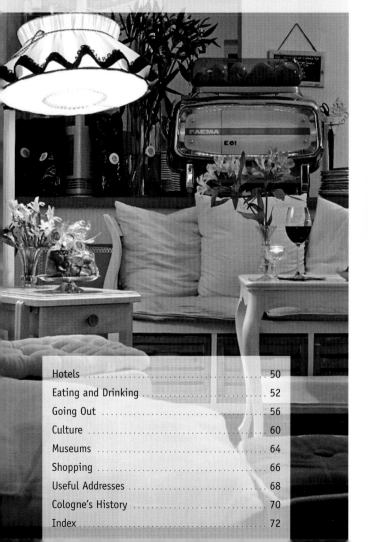

SERVICE

Hotels

FLORA AND BOTANICAL GARDEN

One of the oldest parks in the city is the Flora, next to the zoo. It was laid out in 1864 to plans by Peter Joseph Lenné, the landscape gardener of the royal park in Potsdam, and extended in 1914 by the addition of the Botanical Garden. Among its highlights are the first avenue of palms in Germany, the rose gardens and four connected hothouses,

which are being renovated at present. At the centre of the park with its mature trees, exotic plants, ponds, specialist garden areas and countless botanical species is the restored hall for festivities, newly built on the model of its 19th-century predecessor, including a café and a venue for events.

Im Botanischen Garten
▲ *Zoo/Flora*
◆ *8am until dusk*
Free admission

LOW BUDGET

● **CITY-HOSTEL PATHPOINT COLOGNE**
Allerheiligenstrasse 15 (city centre)
Tel. 0221/13056860
▲ Breslauerplatz
www.jugendherberge.de/ de-de/jugendherbergen/ koeln-pathpoint724/ portraet

Young backpackers from all over the world like this accommodation in a converted church close to Cologne Cathedral.

● **DAS KLEINE STAPELHÄUSCHEN***
Fischmarkt 1–3 (Old Town)
Tel. 0221/2727777
▲ Heumarkt
kleines-stapelhaeuschen.de

A small family hotel in historic surroundings on Fischmarkt.

● **HOSTEL KÖLN****
Marsilstein 29 (city centre)
Tel. 0221/9987760
▲ Rudolfplatz
hostel.ag

A modern hostel in a former office building in a quiet yet central location between Neumarkt and Rudolfplatz.

SUPERIOR

3 日 **TIP** ● **1ST FLOOR KÖLN**
Yorkstrasse 1 (Nippes)
Tel. 0221/99375904
▲ Florastrasse
1stfloorkoeln.com

Boardinghouse with comfortable rooms each individually designed in the fancy quarter Nippes.

● **HOPPER HOTEL ST. ANTONIUS****
Dagobertstrasse 32 (Nordstadt)
Tel. 0221/16600
▲ Ebertplatz
www.hopper.de

In what used to be a charitable institution caring for wandering journeymen, the charm of a historic building is combined with modern art and luxurious amenities.

● **HOTEL CHELSEA**
Jülicher Strasse 1 (Belgisches Viertel)
Tel. 0221/207150
▲ Rudolfplatz
www.hotel-chelsea.de

The Qvest Hotel

Hotel Excelsior Ernst

For over 30 years the Chelsea has provided accommodation for artists, who have left their mark here with their works. Other guests appreciate the individual style of the house.

● **HOTEL STADTPALAIS****
Deutz-Kalker Strasse 52 (Deutz)
Tel. 0221/880420
▲ Deutz Technische Hochschule
www.hotelstadtpalais.de

A first-class hotel in the former Kaiser Wilhelm Baths near the LANXESS arena and trade-fair grounds.

● **HUMBOLDT 1**
Kupfergasse 10 (city centre)
Tel. 0221/27243387
▲ Appellhofplatz
humboldt1.de

A small, owner-run boutique hotel in historic premises with warm personal service.

● **STERN AM RATHAUS***
Bürgerstrasse 6 (Old Town)
Tel. 0221/22251750
▲ Rathaus
www.stern-am-rathaus.de

An extremely pleasant hotel with a personal touch, only a short walk from the cathedral.

● **THE NEW YORKER HOTEL****
Deutz-Mülheimer Strasse 204 (Mülheim)
Tel. 0221/47330
▲ Grünstrasse
www.thenewyorkerhotel.de

A design hotel with sensual puristic rooms, very close to the trade-fair site and the LANXESS arena.

DE LUXE

● **HOTEL EXCELSIOR ERNST*****
Trankgasse 1–5/Domplatz (city centre)
Tel. 0221/2701
▲ Dom/Hbf.
www.excelsiorhotelernst.com/

A stylish grand hotel opposite the cathedral and close to the train station for guests who like exclusive surroundings.

● **HOTEL QVEST*****
Gereonskloster 12 (city centre)
Tel. 0221/2785780
▲ Christophstrasse/Mediapark
www.qvest-hotel.com

An out-of-the-ordinary designer hotel in the former city archive, furnished with classic design items.

ZOOLOGICAL GARDEN

More than 10,000 animals from some 700 species live in the 20-hectare gardens of Cologne zoo, one of the most popular zoos in Germany. With its aquarium and insectarium, rainforest house, huge elephant park and hippodrome, as well as the latest attraction, the Clemenshof, a farmyard in the typical style of the Bergisches Land, it reflects both 160 years of zoological history and the transformation from a menagerie to a modern ark for protecting natural species. Its oldest monument is the former elephant house in Moorish style, dating from 1863.

Riehler Strasse 173
▲ *Zoo/Flora*
◆ *Zoo: 9am-6pm (summer),*
9am-5pm (winter)
Aquarium: 9am-6pm
www.koelnerzoo.de

SERVICE

Restaurants

COLOGNE IN NUMBERS

Cologne is one of four German cities with a population of over a million, making it the biggest on the Rhine. Around 180,000 Cologne residents, including over 57,000 Turks, do not have German nationality. 40 per cent of Cologne citizens are Roman Catholics.

The area of the city is 405 square kilometres, of which 230 square kilometres lie on the left bank and 175 on the right bank of the Rhine. The city boundary is 130 kilometres long. The highest point has an altitude of 118 metres, the lowest 37.5 metres above sea level.

Almost 140 square kilometres are built up; parks and green spaces account for 37 square kilometres; 82 square kilometres are devoted to agriculture; and the city has more than 56 square kilometres of woodland. In Cologne there are over 125,000 residential buildings. The tallest monument is the Colonius TV tower at 243 metres. It has been a city landmark since 1981.

The cathedral is the second-tallest building

● **485 GRAD**
Kyffhäuserstrasse 44
(Kwartier Latäng)
Tel. 0221/39753330
▲ Zülpicher Strasse
◆ Mon-Wed 5pm-10pm,
Thu noon-10pm,
Fri-Sat noon-11pm,
Sun noon-10pm
www.485grad.de

A trendy restaurant that has gone back to the roots of Neapolitan pizza: baked at 485°C in less than 60 seconds. Antipasti and home-made dolci and cake are also on offer.

● **BRASSERIE MARIE**
Zülpicher Strasse 268
(Sülz)
Tel. 0221/96269194
▲ Weyertal
◆ Tue-Sat from 6 pm
www.brasserie-marie.de

Paris feeling in Cologne. A cosy restaurant with outstanding french cuisine in relaxed atmosphere.

● **HORNOCHSE**
Neusser Strasse 304
(Nippes)
Tel. 0221/99758060
▲ Florastrasse
◆ Tue-Sun 12 noon-10pm
hornochse.koeln

A popular burger joint that also serves vegetarian and fish burgers.

● **ENOTECA LA CANTINA**
Marzellenstrasse 45–49
(city centre)
Tel. 0221/123778
▲ Dom/Hbf.
◆ Mon-Sat 10am-3pm,
6-11pm
www.enoteca-la-cantina.de

A small deli with a family atmosphere serving wonderful antipasti, delicious pasta and other Italian specialities, accompanied by selected wines.

● **FÄHRHAUS**
Steinstrasse 1
(Rodenkirchen)
Tel. 0221/9359969
▲ Heinrich-Lübke-Ufer
◆ Mon-Sat 11am-1am,
Sun 10am-1am
www.faehrhauskoeln.de

The trip out to the historic ferry house in Rodenkirchen is worthwhile for its location on the Rhine and excellent Mediterranean dishes.

● **FISCHMARKT**
Am Bollwerk 21
(Old Town)
Tel. 0221/2576330
▲ Dom/Hbf.
◆ 10am-midnight
restaurantfischmarktkoeln. eatbu.com

A culinary attraction in the Old Town for those who enjoy something out of the ordinary, whether fish or meat dishes.

● **MAIBECK**
Am Frankenturm 5
(city centre)
Tel. 0221/96267300
▲ Dom/Hbf.
◆ Tue-Sat 12 noon-3pm,
from 5.30pm, Sun from
12 noon
www.maibeck.de

The highly successful concept here is top-quality cuisine without frills.

● **MAISON BLUE**
Im Ferkulum 18-22
(Südstadt)
▲ Chlodwigplatz
◆ Wed-Sun from 6.30pm
www.maisonblue-koeln.de

A wonderful little brasserie where you can enjoy delicious French specialities and game from the Eifel region.

● **POISSON**
Wolfsstrasse 6–14
(city centre)
Tel. 0221/27736883
▲ Friesenplatz
◆ Tue-Fri 12 noon-3pm,
6-10pm, Sat 12 noon-10pm
www.poisson-restaurant.de

The name tells it all: creative gourmet cuisine with fresh fish and regional ingredients.

● **SCAMPINO**
Deutz-Mülheimer
Strasse 199 (Deutz)
Tel. 0221/618544
▲ Wiener Platz
◆ 12 noon-2pm,
6pm-midnight
www.scampino.de

A rendezvous for lovers of Mediterranean fish dishes by the Mülheim harbour.

● **ZIPPIRI**
Riehler Strasse 73
(Nordstadt)
Tel. 0221/92299584
▲ Reichenspergerplatz
◆ Mon, Wed-Sun
6-10.30pm,
Sun noon-2pm
www.zippiri.de

The wine bar and restaurant Zippiri, which means rosemary in Sardinia, serves Italian meals with a Sardinian touch.

in Cologne – its towers reach a height of 157 metres. The tallest skyscraper is the Köln-Turm in the Mediapark at 148 metres, and the tallest on the right bank of the Rhine is the KölnTriangle (103 metres).

With 19 institutions of higher education and approx. 100,000 students, Cologne is one of the three main university cities in Germany. For the media business Cologne is at the top, with six TV broadcasters and over 300 production companies. In the fields of art and culture, the city is also well provided for, with 40 museums and more than 110 galleries.

Cafés

● **CAFÉ BAUTURM**
Aachener Strasse 24–26
(Belgisches Viertel)
▲ Rudolfplatz
◆ Mon-Fri 8am-3am,
Sat-Sun 9am-3am
www.cafe-bauturm.de

Breakfast all day – exis-
tentialist with a cup of
coffee and a cigarette,
or more luxurious with
Prosecco.

● **CAFÉ CENTRAL**
Jülicher Strasse 1
(Belgisches Viertel)
▲ Friesenplatz
◆ Mon-Thu 7am-midnight,
Fri-Sat 7am-1pm,
Sun 8am-11pm
www.cafecentralcologne.de

Outdoors beneath the
palms or in the black-
and-white artists' café,
you can spend the whole
day here, and sometimes
stay for live music in the
evening.

● **CAFÉ FRANCK**
Eichendorffstrasse 30
(Ehrenfeld)
▲ Subbelrather Strasse/
Gürtel
◆ Tue-Sun 10am-7pm,
Shibuya-Lounge:
Fri-Sat from 7pm (Sept-May)
www.cafe-franck.de/

A Cologne institution, for
delicious cream cakes dur-

ing the day and creative
cocktails in the evening.

● **EISCAFE DOLCE
& GELATO**
Pfeilstrasse 51 (city centre)
▲ Rudolfplatz
◆ Mon-Sat 11am-11pm,
Sun 11am-midnight
www.dolce-gelato-nanni.de

Vanilla and chocolate
in traditional style, or
perhaps zuppa inglese
or pink grapefruit – this
family-run ice-cream par-
lour is one of the best in
Cologne.

● **FASSBENDER KÖLN**
Obenmarspforten 7
(Old Town)
▲ Heumarkt
◆ Mon-Fri 9am-6.30pm,
Sat 9am-7pm, Sun 11am-6pm
www.fassbender.de

The circular room in 1950s style is an architectural attraction, and the charm of that era lives on here.

● KAFFEESAPIENS
Charles-de-Gaulle-Platz 1 (Deutz)
▲ Messe Deutz
◆ Mon-Fri 8am-5.30pm
kaffeesapiens.com

A temple to coffee-drinking, with its own coffee blends, directly sourced. Farmers from the region supply the milk, and there are hearty sandwiches.

● LEUCHTE KAFFEEBAR
Karolingerring 21 (Südstadt)
◆ Chlodwigplatz
◆ Mon-Fri 7.30am-7pm
Sat-Sun 8.30am-7pm

In this café on two levels, lovingly furnished in retro style, you can eat home-made cake and tasty quiches, all of it organic, fair-trade and regional.

● PRINTEN SCHMITZ
Breite Strasse 87 (city centre)
▲ Appellhofplatz
◆ Mon-Fri 8.30am-7pm,
Sat 8.30am-6pm
www.printenschmitz.com

An old-established Cologne café with a tempting array of cakes. The house speciality is Printen, a kind of gingerbread. A large one in the shape of Cologne Cathedral makes a good souvenir.

● SALON SCHMITZ
Aachener Strasse 28 (Belgisches Viertel)
▲ Rudolfplatz
◆ From 9am
salonschmitz.com

For the first espresso of the day, quiche for lunch or a last drink in the evening, Salon Schmitz is always a good place to go.

● THE COFFEE GANG
Hohenstaufenring 19 (city centre)
▲ Zülpicher Platz
◆ Tue-Fri 8am-6pm,
Sat 9.30am-6pm,
Sun 11am-6pm
www.thecoffeegang.de

Coffee and espresso bar serving fair-trade products, freshly roasted. For the hungry there are New York cheesecakes and other homemade cakes or bread, pesto, tapenade and grilled vegetables.

● TÖRTCHEN TÖRTCHEN
Apostelnstrasse 19 (city centre)
▲ Rudolfplatz
◆ Mon-Sat 9am-7pm,
Sun 10am-6pm
www.toertchentoertchen.de

This pink and white shop and café is heaven if you love extravagant French patisserie.

COLOGNE CALENDAR

JUNE
★ Summer entertainment:
www.sommerkoeln.de

JULY
★ Fireworks on the Rhine:
www.koelner-lichter.de
★ ColognePride
(CSD street festival):
www.colognepride.de
★ Summer festival:
www.bb-promotion.com/koelner-sommerfestival
★ Summerjam (reggae festival): *summerjam.de*

AUGUST
★ c/o pop (Cologne Music Festival): *c-o-pop.de*
★ Gamescom (leading fair for interactive games and entertainment):
www.gamescom.de

SEPTEMBER
★ Photokina (leading global fair for imaging and video):
www.photokina.de

OCTOBER
★ Köln Comedy Festival:
koelncomedy.de
★ Cologne Marathon:
koeln-marathon.de

NOVEMBER
★ Short-film festival Köln:
kffk.de

DECEMBER
★ Christmas markets:
www.koelntourismus.de

SERVICE

Pubs, beer cellars & beer gardens

THE KÖLSCH MENU

Menus printed in dialect (Kölsch, the same as the word for the local beer) list regional specialities, mostly hearty dishes with names that need explanation even for German visitors to Cologne.

Ääppelschloot
Potato salad

Brodwoosch
Bratwurst, fried sausage

Hämmche
Pork knuckle, served with mashed potato and sauerkraut

Halve Hahn
A rye-bread roll with a slice of mature Dutch cheese, butter and mustard

Himmel un Äd
Fried Flönz (black pudding) with mashed potato and apple sauce

Kölsche Kaviar
Black pudding with onion rings

Rievkoche
Fried potato cakes like rösti

Soorbrode
Sour-marinated roast beef or horse meat

● **ALCAZAR**
Bismarckstrasse 39 a
(Belgisches Viertel)
Tel. 0221/515733
▲ Friesenplatz
◆ Mon-Fri from 12 noon, Sat from 6pm, Sun from 5pm
www.alcazar-koeln.de

Thanks to its varied menu at reasonable prices and pleasant atmosphere, what was once a student pub has kept its popularity for decades.

● **BOOTSHAUS "ALTE LIEBE"**
Rodenkirchener Leinpfad (Rodenkirchen)
Tel. 0221/392361
▲ Uferstrasse
◆ From 11am (summer), Tue-Fri from 11am, Sat-Sun from 12 noon (winter)
www.bootshaus-alte-liebe.de

The "Old Love" is a houseboat with a beer garden and a great view of the Rhine and Rodenkirchen.

● **BRÜSSELER**
Brüsseler Platz 1
(Belgisches Viertel)
Tel. 0221/96028921
▲ Friedensplatz
◆ Mon-Thu 3pm-1am, Fri-Sat 12 noon-3am, Sun 3pm-1am
www.bruesseler-koeln.de

A pub on Brüsseler Platz for young and old. The interior blends industrial

design with clerical items, outside you can watch the comings and goings on the square.

● **FILOS**
Merowingerstrasse 42
(Südstadt)
Tel. 0221/329147
▲ Chlodwigplatz
◆ Sun-Thu 9am-1am, Fri-Sat 9am-3am
www.filoskoeln.de

A Südstadt institution, open for breakfast and late cocktails.

● **GILDEN IM ZIMS**
Heumarkt 77 (city centre)
Tel. 0221/16866110
▲ Heumarkt
◆ Mon-Fri 12 noon-1am, Sat 11am-3am, Sun 11am-11pm
www.haus-zims.de

A hip Brauhaus pub in a historic building!

● **HEISING & ADELMANN**
Friesenstrasse 58-60
(Friesenviertel)
Tel. 0221/1309424

▲ Friesenplatz
◆ Tue-Sat from 6pm
www.heising-und-adelmann.de

A trendy restaurant in the Friesenviertel, where guests often party until the early hours.

● KM 689–COLOGNE BEACH CLUB

Rheinparkweg (Deutz)
Tel. 0221/65004310
▲ Bahnhof Deutz
◆ Fri-Sun from 12 noon, Mon-Thu from 4pm (summer)
www.km689.de

On 3,500 square metres of fine-grained sand you can watch the sun go down behind the Cologne skyline or just chill out to your heart's content.

● LOMMERZHEIM

Siegesstrasse 18 (Deutz)
Tel. 0221/814392
▲ Deutzer Freiheit
◆ Mon, Wed-Fri 11am-2pm, 4.30pm-1am, Sat-Sun from 10.30am
www.paeffgen-koelsch.de/gastronomien

A pub on the right bank with cult status, antlers on the walls and a creaking wooden floor. The thick, juicy pork chops are legendary.

● MAINZER HOF

Mainzer Strasse/Maternusstrasse 18 (Südstadt)
Tel. 0221/312549
▲ Ubierring
◆ from 5pm
www.mainzerhof-koeln.de

The "Südstadt living room" serves delicious food and is a good place to watch the sun set.

● METRONOM

Weyerstrasse 59 (city centre)
Tel. 0221/213465
▲ Barbarossaplatz
◆ Sun-Thu 8pm-1am, Fri-Sat 8pm-3am
www.metronom.koeln

A rare jazz pub, an essential part of the Cologne jazz scene for over 40 years.

● PÄFFGEN BRAUHAUS

Friesenstrasse 64–66 (Friesenviertel)
Tel. 0221/135461
▲ Friesenplatz
◆ Sun-Thu 10am-midnight, Fri-Sat 10am-0.30am
www.paeffgen-koelsch.de

The home of a brewery, where the Päffgen family have brewed with water from their own well for 120 years. Don't expect it to be modern and shiny inside, but with its pleasant beer garden, heated and covered in winter, this is the city's most authentic Brauhaus (brewpub).

● STADTGARTEN

Venloer Strasse 40 (Belgisches Viertel)
Tel. 0221/9529940
▲ Friesenplatz
◆ 12 noon-midnight (in good weather)
www.stadtgarten.de

One of Cologne's most popular beer gardens attracts a mixed crowd.

BEWARE OF THE WAITER!

When drinking in a Brauhaus, you need to observe certain rules! The waiter here is called a "Köbes" (from the name Jakob), and the tool of his trade is a round tray from which he places a

glass of Kölsch on the table, unasked. His uniform is a long apron and a blue knitted cardigan. He is characterised by a ready tongue, and it is pointless to try to argue with him.

SERVICE

Bars & Nightlife

Little Link

FIREWORKS ON THE RHINE

Almost a million visitors come to Cologne on a Saturday in July to see the Rhine turned into a sea of flames and colour. The event, Kölner Lichter, begins in the afternoon with a programme of entertainment at the Tanzbrunnen,

and the fireworks display starts when darkness falls. The overture to this is a parade of 50 illuminated ships, accompanied by fireworks, from the suburb of Porz to the city centre, where spectators greet them by waving hundreds of thousands of sparklers. The climax is Germany's biggest display of rising fireworks with synchronised music. They go off for 30 minutes from two 120-metre-long boats moored between the Hohenzollern Bridge and Tanzbrunnen.

www.koelner-lichter.de

● **DIE KUNSTBAR**
Chargesheimer Platz 1
(next to the central station, opposite the Alter Wartesaal/city centre)
▲ Dom/Hbf.
◆ Tue-Thu from 7 pm,
Fri-Sat from 8pm
www.diekunstbar.de

Here cocktails join an annually changing exhibition of works by an artist.

● **HEINZ GAUL**
Vogelsanger Strasse 197
(Ehrenfeld)
▲ Venloer Strasse/Gürtel
◆ Fri-Sat from 11pm
heinzgaul.de

A small club in an old building, where electro and hip-hop sounds boom out.

● **KÖNIGSWASSER**
Limburger Strasse 23
(Belgisches Viertel)
▲ Friesenplatz
◆ From 10pm
www.koenigswasser.de

A revival of a legendary club with two dance floors and scope for the young artistic scene to be creative.

● **LITTLE LINK**
Maastrichter Strasse 20
(Belgisches Viertel)
▲ Friesenplatz
◆ Mon-Sat from 7pm
www.littlelink.de

A stylish bar and lounge with naked brick walls and innovative drinks.

● **MONKEY BAR**
(in 25hours Hotel
The Circle)
Im Klapperhof 22-24
(Friesenviertel)
◆ Sun-Wed 5pm-1am,
Thu-Sat 5pm-2am
www.25hours-hotels.com/
restaurants-bars/koeln/
monkey-bar

The rooftop bar is an ideal spot for communication and popular for its cocktail and long drink creations.

● **ONA MOR**
Roonstrasse 94
(Kwartier Latäng)
▲ Zülpicher Platz
◆ From 8pm
www.onamor.de

A lovely cocktail bar with lots of its own recipes.

● **PIANO BAR**
(in the Hotel Excelsior)
Domplatz/Trankgasse 1–5
▲ Dom/Hbf.
◆ 11am-1am
www.excelsiorhotelernst.com/
restaurants-bar/
piano-bar.html

For home-made cakes and sweets at teatime or cocktails in the evening with discreet piano music, this place next to Cologne Cathedral is a good retreat.

● **SCHÄLSICK BAR**
(in the Hyatt Regency)
Kennedy-Ufer 2 a (Deutz)
▲ Bahnhof Deutz
◆ 11am-1am
cologne.regency.hyatt.
com/de/hotel/dining/
SchälsickBarandTerrace.
html

A popular place for a drink on the right bank of the Rhine, with a choice from more than 60 different kinds of whisky.

● **SEIBERT'S**
Fliesenwall 33
(Friesenviertel)
▲ Friesenplatz
◆ Tue-Sun 5pm-2am
seiberts-bar.com

A classic bar in a historic building with a wonderful garden terrace in the courtyard.

● **SIXPACK**
Aachener Strasse 33
(Belgisches Viertel)
▲ Rudolfplatz
◆ From 8pm
www.facebook.com/
sixpack.bar.cologne

A legend in Cologne's nightlife, serving many different sorts of bottled beer.

● **SPIRITS**
Engelbertstrasse 63
(Belgisches Viertel)
▲ Zülpicher Platz
◆ Mon-Thu 8pm-2am,
Fri-Sat 8pm-3am
www.spiritsbar.de

A trendy joint in the Belgisches Viertel, where the surroundings, drinks, service and sound are all just right.

● **TSUNAMI**
Im Ferkulum 9
(Severinsviertel)
▲ Chlodwigplatz
◆ From 8pm
www.tsunami-club.de

Music club with indie, punk rock, rock 'n' roll and more, but not mainstream.

C/O POP FESTIVAL

In August international stars, celebrated newcomers and up-and-coming unknowns come to Cologne's music venues when the c/o pop festival gets going. For five days, more than 80 bands, artists and DJs can be heard in over 30 different concert halls, clubs, bars and open-air venues, both in the city centre and further out. For more than ten

years this music festival for electronic pop music has been an established feature of the event calendar. At the same time a specialist event for the latest issues in the business, the c/o pop Convention, and SoundTrack_Cologne, the biggest German congress for music and sound in film, games and media, take place.

c-o-pop.de
www.soundtrackcologne.de

Culture

GÜRZENICH ORCHESTRA

Robert and Clara Schumann played with this orchestra, Giuseppe Verdi and Richard Wagner conducted their latest works with it, Richard Strauss chose it for the world première of *Till Eulenspiegel* (1895) and *Don Quixote* (1898), Gustav Mahler for his 5th symphony. The list of principal conductors ranges from Conradin Kreutzer and Hermann Abendroth to Markus Stenz and, at present, François-Xavier Roth. Named after the festival hall in which it performed for decades, today the Gürzenich-Orchester is one Germany's

longest-established symphony orchestras. Its base is the Philharmonie in Cologne, and it plays for the Cologne opera. Its project "GO live!", in which performances in the Philharmonie are recorded live and can be purchased immediately after the concert, is unique worldwide.

www.guerzenich-orchester.de

THEATRE

● ARTHEATER
Ehrenfeldgürtel 127 (Ehrenfeld)
Tel. 0221/5503344
▲ Subbelrather Strasse/ Gürtel
artheater.info/11/

A young theatre that aims to stage dramatic work of different cultures and styles under one roof.

● ATELIER THEATER
Roonstrasse 78 (Kwartier Latäng)
Tel. 0221/242485
▲ Zülpicher Platz
ateliertheater.de

A small basement theatre with an innovative cabaret programme directed by the satirist Rosa K. Wirtz.

● BÜHNE DER KULTUREN
Platenstrasse 32 (Ehrenfeld)
Tel. 0221/9559510
▲ Subbelrather Strasse/ Gürtel
www.buehnederkulturen.de

Members of the ensemble are of various nationalities and religions, and wish to convey this cultural diversity by artistic means.

● COMEDIA COLONIA
Vondelstrasse 4–8 (Südstadt)
Tel. 0221/88877222
▲ Chlodwigplatz, Ulrepforte
www.comedia-koeln.de/

With a love of experimentation and a programme of cabaret and satire that has a national reputation, the Comedia is well-known beyond the city of Cologne.

● ERSTES KÖLNER WOHNZIMMERTHEATER
Probsteigasse 21 (city centre)
Tel. 0221/1300707
▲ Christophstrasse/ Mediapark
www.wohnzimmertheater.de

A small venue for comedy, drama and cabaret.

● FREIES WERKSTATT-THEATER
Zugweg 10 (Südstadt)
Tel. 0221/327817
▲ Chlodwigplatz
www.fwt-koeln.de

Known for 20 years for its work in experimental theatre.

● HÄNNESCHEN-THEATER
Eisenmarkt 2–4 (Old Town)
Tel. 0221/2581201
▲ Heumarkt
www.haenneschen.de

The puppets speaking Cologne dialect have been a local institution for 200 years – unfortunately almost always sold out.

● HORIZONT THEATER

Thürmchenswall 25
(Nordstadt)
Tel. 0221/131604
▲ Ebertplatz
www.horizont-theater.de

One of the city's best-known and most renowned independent theatres, with a programme characterised by humour and delight in acting, on a basement stage at the heart of the city.

● KLÜNGELPÜTZ

Gertrudenstrasse 24
(city centre)
Tel. 0152/04443368
▲ Neumarkt
kluengelpuetz.de

Sharp and witty political satire.

● SCHAUSPIELHAUS

Schanzenstrasse 6–20
(Mülheim)
Tel. 0221/22128400
▲ Keupstrasse
www.schauspiel.koeln

The municipal theatre company directed by Stefan Bachmann plays on the Carlswerk site. Its programme ranges from classic and contemporary

dramas to theatrical treatments of current issues in society.

● SENFTÖPFCHEN

Grosse Neugasse 2–4
(Old Town)
Tel. 0221/2581058
▲ Dom/Hbf.
www.senftoepfchen-theater.de

For over 40 years a popular venue for cabaret, chansons and other small-scale performances, where relatively unknown performers are given the chance to shine.

● STUDIOBÜHNE KÖLN

Universitätsstrasse 16 a
(Sülz)
Tel. 0221/4704513
▲ Universität
studiobuehnekoeln.de

Germany's oldest university theatre is known for its experimental style and visits by touring companies.

● THEATER AM DOM

Glockengasse 11
(city centre)
Tel. 0221/2580153
▲ Neumarkt
www.theateramdom.de

Comedy and farce, with guest appearances by well-known actors.

● THEATER DER KELLER

Kleingedankstrasse 6
(Südstadt)
Tel. 0221/318059
▲ Ulrepforte
www.theater-der-keller.de

The oldest independent theatre in Cologne devotes itself to contemporary works.

INTERNATIONAL COMEDY FESTIVAL

For stand-up comedy and variety performances, for musical and literary cabaret, for the last 25 years the biggest comedy festival in Germany has been held in Cologne in October. More than 150 artists, both stars and unknown newcomers, present a diverse programme of outstandingly good entertainment in more than 100 shows at some 20 venues over a two-week period. The festival kicks off with its legendary opening show "Cologne lacht!" (laughs). One of the highlights is the 1Live Köln Comedy-Nacht XXL – Europe's biggest comedy show. During the festival the Deutscher Comedy-Preis is awarded in various categories in the Coloneum, an event that is later broadcast live on the RTL the TV channel.

www.koeln-comedy.de

SERVICE

Culture

LIT.COLOGNE

The absolute highlight of the year in the city's literature scene is Lit.Cologne, which has taken place each year since 2001. It is Europe's biggest literary festival, attracting large audiences, including well-attended readings and discussions in English with major English-speaking authors. Lasting eleven days, it con-

sists of more than 175 events at a variety of venues, with over 200 authors and artists. The programme is a high-calibre mix of international and German-language literature, from bestsellers to newcomers. A feature is the encounter of authors with artists from different disciplines. Lit.Kid is a series of cultural events for children with almost 90 performances.

www.litcologne.de

● THEATER IM BAUTURM
Aachener Strasse 24
(Belgisches Viertel)
Tel. 0221/524242
▲ Rudolfplatz
www.theater-im-bauturm.de

A contemporary theatre with literary ambitions that stages a diverse, high-quality programme with its own productions.

● THEATER TIEFROT
Dagobertstrasse 32
(Nordstadt)
Tel. 0221/4600911
▲ Ebertplatz
www.theater-tiefrot.com

A small private theatre run by the actor and director Volker Lippmann in the cellar vault of the Hopper Hotel St. Antonius.

● VOLKSBÜHNE AM RUDOLFPLATZ
Aachener Strasse 5
(Belgisches Viertel)
Tel. 0221/251747
▲ Rudolfplatz
www.volksbuehne-rudolfplatz.de

The famous Volkstheater Millowitsch plays in Cologne's oldest theatre. At other times the stage is free for music, political satire, comedy and cabaret.

MUSIC

● ALTES PFANDHAUS
Kartäuserwall 20
(Südstadt)
Tel. 0221/2783685
▲ Chlodwigplatz
www.altes-pfandhaus.de

● HOCHSCHULE FÜR MUSIK UND TANZ
Unter Krahnenbäumen 87
(Nordstadt)
Tel. 0221/9128180
▲ Ebertplatz
www.mhs-koeln.de

Frequently the students put on high-quality performances of classical music and jazz.

● LOFT
Wissmannstrasse 30
(Ehrenfeld)
Tel. 0221/9521555
▲ Körnerstrasse
www.loftkoeln.de

A venue for improvised music, contemporary music and jazz on one floor of a converted factory.

● MUSICAL DOME
Goldgasse 1/Breslauer Platz (city centre)
Tel. 0221/73440
▲ Breslauer Platz
www.mehr.de

In the big blue tent behind the central station, productions of various musicals are staged.

● OPER DER STADT KÖLN
Rheinparkweg 1 (Deutz)
Tel. 0221/22128400
▲ Bahnhof Deutz
www.oper.koeln

The city opera ensemble is currently performing in the Staatenhaus on the right bank while the opera house is renovated.

● PHILHARMONIE
Bischofsgartenstrasse 1 (city centre)
Tel. 0221/280280
▲ Dom/Hbf.
www.koelner-philharmonie.de

Modelled on an amphitheatre, this concert hall is known for its outstanding architecture and excellent acoustics, as well as for the quality of its programme.

CINEMAS

● CINEDOM
Im Mediapark 1 (Nordstadt)
Tel. 0221/95195555
▲ Christophstrasse/ Mediapark
www.cinedom.de

A big, modern multiplex cinema with the latest projection and sound technology, where all the latest mainstream movies are screened.

● FILMPALETTE
Lübecker Strasse 15 (Nordstadt)
Tel. 0221/122112
▲ Ebertplatz
www.filmpalette-koeln.de

This 80-seater screens low-budget productions, and is a forum for trash films and art films.

● METROPOLIS
Ebertplatz 19 (Nordstadt)
Tel. 0221/7391245
▲ Ebertplatz
metropolis-koeln.de

English-language films can be seen here in the original version. It is also a venue for premieres and good children's cinema.

LITERATURE

● LITERATURHAUS KÖLN E.V.
Grosser Griechenmarkt 39 (city centre)
Tel. 0221/9955580
▲ Poststrasse
literaturhaus-koeln.de

Debutants and holders of the Nobel Prize for Literature, authors and readers of children's books and contemporary literature meet here for varied activities.

MEDIAPARK

One of Cologne's most prominent urban development projects of the 1990s is the Mediapark on the site of old railway freight yards. Embedded in a park landscape with a lake are companies and educational institutions from the fields of media, IT, culture, education, medicine, research and trade, as well as a hotel, shops, restaurants, the city's first multiplex cinema and housing. Planned by the Canadian architect Eberhard Zedier, and radiating from a central open space, is an architectural ensemble of seven-storey buildings and the 148-metre-high KölnTurm with a façade by Jean Nouvel that reflects the panorama of Cologne.

www.mediapark.de

Museums

KUNST. DESIGN IM DIALOG

MUSEUM SCHNÜTGEN

What more effective place could there be to present Christian art than the interior of a Romanesque basilica? St Cäcilien, once a collegiate church, is a unique setting for masterpieces from more than 800 years that provide insights into the life and thought of the Middle Ages and tell fascinating stories. In the church and a new exhibition space in the Kulturquartier on Neumarkt, visitors can learn about the radiance and the message of stained glass windows, about how art was converted to gold with the famous Golden Panel from St Ursula as an example, or about the medieval trade in paper-maché copies and clay-pipe miniatures of well-known saints' images.

Cäcilienstrasse 29–33
(city centre)
Tel. 0221/22131355
▲ *Poststrasse*
◆ *Tue-Sun 10am-6pm,*
Thu until 8pm
www.museum-schnuetgen.de

● **DUFTMUSEUM (PERFUME)**
➤ p. 16

● **EL-DE-HAUS**
(NS-Documentation Center)
Appellhofplatz 23–25
(city centre)
Tel. 0221/22126331
▲ Appellhofplatz
◆ Tue-Fri 10am-6pm, Sat-Sun 11am-6pm, first Thu in the month 10am-10pm
www.museenkoeln.de/ns-dokumentationszentrum

Exhibition on Cologne under National Socialism.

● **KÄTHE-KOLLWITZ-MUSEUM**
Neumarkt 18–24
(city centre)
Tel 0221/2272899
▲ Neumarkt
◆ Tue-Fri 10am-6pm, Sat-Sun 11am-6pm, guided tours Sun 3pm, Thu 5pm
www.kollwitz.de

The world's biggest collection of the art of Käthe Kollwitz.

● **KÖLNER KARNEVALS-MUSEUM**
Maarweg 134–136
(Braunsfeld)
Tel. 0221/574000
▲ Maarweg
◆ For opening times see: *www.koelnerkarnevals museum.de*

The museum examines Carnival as a cultural phenomenon and its practices.

● **KÖLNISCHES STADTMUSEUM**
Zeughausstrasse 1–3
(city centre)
Tel. 0221/22125789
▲ Appellhofplatz
◆ Tue 10am-8pm, Wed-Sun 10am-5pm, first Thu in the month 10am-10pm, guided tours Sat 2.30pm, Sun 11.15am
www.museenkoeln.de/ksm

The history, intellectual, economic and everyday life of Cologne.

● **KOLUMBA** ➤ p. 32

● **KUNSTSTATION ST. PETER**
Leonhard-Tietz-Strasse 6
(city centre)
Tel. 0221/9213030
▲ Neumarkt
◆ Wed-Fri 12 noon-4pm, Sat-Sun 1-5pm
www.sankt-peter-koeln.de

A dialogue between a church and art, between art and religion.

● **KUNSTVEREIN**
Hahnenstrasse 6
(city centre)
Tel. 0221/217021
▲ Rudolfplatz
◆ Tue-Sun 11am-6pm
koelnischerkunstverein.de

The purpose of the association is to promote contemporary art.

● **MUSEUM DES DEUTSCHEN TANZ-ARCHIVS KÖLN**
Im Mediapark 7 (3rd floor) (Nordstadt)
Tel. 0221/88595400
▲ Christophstrasse/ Mediapark
◆ Thu-Tue 2-7pm
www.sk-kultur.de

Exhibition about the history of dance.

● **MUSEUM FÜR ANGEWANDTE KUNST**
An der Rechtschule (city centre)
Tel. 0221/22126714
▲ Dom/Hbf.
◆ Tue-Sun 11am-5pm, first Thu in the month 11am-10pm, guided tours Wed 11am, Sat + Sun 2.30pm
www.museenkoeln.de/ museum-fuer-angewandte-kunst

European arts and crafts from the Middle Ages to the present.

● **MUSEUM LUDWIG**
➤ p. 46

● **MUSEUM FÜR OSTASIATISCHE KUNST**
Universitätsstrasse 100 (Lindenthal)
Tel. 0221/22128608
▲ Universitätsstrasse
◆ Tue-Sun 11am-5pm, first Thu in the month 11am-10pm
www.museen koeln.de/mok

Collections of Chinese, Japanese and Korean art.

● **ODYSSEUM**
Corintostrasse 1 (Kalk)
Tel. 0221/69068111
▲ Kalk Post, Trimborn-strasse
◆ Tue-Fri 9am-6pm, Sat-Sun 10am-7pm
www.odysseum.de

An interactive science adventure park for the whole family.

● **RAUTENSTRAUCH-JOEST-MUSEUM**
Cäcilienstrasse 29–33 (city centre)
Tel. 0221/22131356
▲ Neumarkt
◆ Tue-Wed, Fri-Sun 10am-6pm, Thu 10am-8pm
www.museenkoeln.de/ rautenstrauch-joest-museum

Exhibitions about life in non-European cultures.

● **RÖMISCH-GERMA-NISCHES MUSEUM**
Roncalliplatz 4 (city centre)
Tel. 0221/22124438 und 22124590
▲ Dom/Hbf.
◆ Tue-Sun 10am-5pm, first Thu in the month 11am-10pm
www.museenkoeln.de/ roemisch-germanisches-museum/

Daily life in Roman Cologne.

● **SCHOKOLADEN-MUSEUM** ➤ p. 40

● **SPORT- UND OLYM-PIAMUSEUM** ➤ p. 41

● **WALLRAF-RICH-ARTZ-MUSEUM** ➤ p. 47

SCULPTURE PARK

The Skulpturenpark close to the zoo is a special place to take a walk. The exhibition entitled *KölnSkulptur* with its changing works presents trends in contemporary sculpture, seeing this art as an idea that relates to the existing situation. It is a place that gives

Sculpture by Amalia Ulman

visitors time – time to linger, moments to contemplate a range of different materials. The present exhibition of contemporary works, the eighth so far, goes back to a private initiative by the collectors Michael and Eleonore Stoffel.

Main entrance: Riehler Strasse (near Zoobrücke)
▲ Zoo/Flora
◆ 10.30am-7pm (April-Sept) 10.30am-5pm (Oct-March)
www.skulpturen parkkoeln.de

Shopping

EAU DE COLOGNE

Not many people know that eau de Cologne used to be a panacea for all ills. Inhaled, drunk or worn on the skin, it was thought to be a protection against plague. An "aqua admirabile" (miracle water) was produced in Cologne as long ago as the late 17th century, but it was not until French army officers used it to counteract the bad smells in the city during the Seven Years' War (1756–63) that a medicinal product came to be used as a perfume under a name now known worldwide: eau de Cologne.

● 4711-HAUS
Glockengasse 4
(city centre)
▲ Appellhofplatz
◆ Mon-Fri 9.30am-6.30pm, Sat 9.30am-6pm
www.4711.com

Here you can buy all the perfume products of the 4711 brand and also sample this famous eau de Cologne from a fountain.

● ADIEU TRISTESSE
Moltkestrasse 85
(Belgisches Viertel)
▲ Moltkestrasse
◆ Mon-Fri 12 noon-6pm, Sat 12 noon-4pm
www.adieutristesse.eu

Soft toys, cushions and children's clothing – everything on sale here is a one-off, yet these unique products, made with love, are affordable.

● BÄRENDRECK APOTHEKE
Richard-Wagner-Strasse 1
(city centre)
▲ Rudolfplatz
◆ Tue-Fri 12 noon-6.30pm, Sat 12 noon-4.30pm
www.baerendreck-apotheke.de

Everything to do with liquorice, from liquorice mustard to liquorice soap and toothpaste, and more than 600 kinds of liquorice to eat.

● BUCHHANDLUNG WALTER KÖNIG
Ehrenstrasse 4
(city centre)
▲ Friesenplatz
◆ Mon-Sat 10am-7pm
www.buchhandlung-walther-koenig

You can recognise this exquisite bookshop by the "tumbling books" on its corner building. A veritable paradise for bibliophiles, who can find books about art, architecture, photography, cinema, fashion and design.

● DIE TAGEDIEBE
Hirschgässchen 1
(Südstadt)
▲ Ubierring
◆ Mon-Fri 11am-7pm, Sat 10am-6pm
www.die-tagediebe.com

Books and many other beautiful things.

● **DIE WERKSTATT**
An der Eiche 9
(Südstadt)
▲ Chlodwigplatz
◆ Mon-Fri 12 noon-7pm,
Sat 11am-3pm
www.die-werkstatt-koeln.de

Porcelain jewellery and
home accessories are
made here.

● **DOMSHOP**
Roncalliplatz
(city centre)
▲ Dom/Hbf.
◆ Mon-Sat 10am-7pm
www.der-koelnshop.de

For a cast of a gargoyle,
a cookie-cutter, biscuits
in the shape of the
cathedral tower or a
rosary – buy here to
support the cathedral.

Kölner Dom
5.– EUR

● **HERNANDO CORTEZ
SCHOKOLADEN**
Gertrudenstrasse 23
(city centre)
▲ Friesenplatz
◆ Mon-Sat 10am-8pm
(May-Aug until 7pm)
www.hernando-cortez.de

Here you can order a cup
of drinking chocolate and
buy the finest chocolate
from all around the world.

● **HONIG MÜNGERSDORFF**
An St. Agatha 37
(city centre)
▲ Heumarkt
◆ Mon-Fri 8am-1pm,
2-6pm, Sat 9am-1pm
www.honig-muengersdorff.de

For over 150 years this
specialist shop has sold
everything connected
with honey, from mead to
honey sweets and liqueur.

● **KÖLNSHOP**
(in Kölntourismus)
Kardinal-Höffner-Platz 1
(city centre)
▲ Dom/Hbf.
◆ Mon-Sat 9am-8pm,
Sun 10am-5pm
www.der-koelnshop.de

For fruit gums in the
shape of the cathedral or
a Cologne egg-timer, for
local souvenires the shop
in the tourist office is a
good source!

● **LOFT 43**
Marzellenstrasse 43
(city centre)
▲ Dom/Hbf.
◆ Tue-Fri 12 noon-8pm,
Sat 2-8pm
www.loft43.eu

Vintage furniture covering
decades of design from
the 1920s to the 1980s.

● **MAUS & CO.**
Breite Strasse 6–26/
WDR-Arkaden (city centre)
▲ Appellhofplatz
◆ Mon-Fri 10am-7pm,
Sat 10am-6pm
www.wdrshop.de/maus-co

This is the merchandis-
ing outlet for all kinds of
products associated with
popular characters from
the programmes of the
broadcaster WDR, includ-
ing the Mouse and Captain
Bluebear.

koelnmesse

TRADE FAIRS

On the right bank of
the Rhine, behind the
80-metre-tall tower (Mes-
seturm) and the historic
trade-fair halls now oc-
cupied by the RTL broad-
caster, lie the grounds of
Kölnmesse, the world's
fourth-biggest trade-fair
site, with 11 exhibition
halls covering 284,000
square metres and
100,000 square metres of
open space. Around three
million visitors from over
200 countries and some
50,000 exhibitors from
more than 120 countries
come here every year
to take part in over 80
specialist trade shows in
more 25 business sectors,
including leading global
fairs.

www.koelnmesse.de

Useful Addresses

"WE'RE GOING TO FC KÖLLE ..."

... means a trip to the stadium of 1. FC Köln – Cologne Football Club, founded in 1948. It may not be as old as some other German clubs, but has a great tradition. Hennes Weisweiler, Wolfgang Overath and Bernd Schuster are just a few of the famous players who have trodden the turf here. 1. FC Köln won the first-ever Bundesliga champion-

ship and put its stamp on German professional football for many years. The most remarkable thing about the club are its fans. It is not easy to get hold of a season ticket, and even when the team is not performing well, the loyalty of the fans in the Rhein-energie-Stadion is not shaken. At every home game they sing their favourite anthem, with the words "We're true to you, FC Kölle".

www.fc.de

INFORMATION

KÖLNTOURISMUS GMBH
Kardinal-Höffner-Platz 1
50667 Köln
Tel. 0221/346430
◆ Mon-Sat 9am-8pm,
Sun 10am-5pm
www.koelntourismus.de

ARRIVAL/DEPARTURE

● **BY AIR:** Cologne-Bonn Airport lies east of Cologne, about 17 kilometres from the city centre.
Tel. 02203/404001
For the latest information about departures and arrivals, see the website
www.koeln-bonn-airport.de

LOCAL TRAINS (S-BAHN): lines 13 (destination Köln-Ehrenfeld) and 19 (destination Horrem) and regional trains RE 8 and RE 6a go to Cologne's central station in approx. 15 minutes. For further connections to intercity, regional express and local trains, refer to
www.koeln-bonn-airport.de/parken-anreise/bus-bahn.html

TAXI: taxi ranks are next to the exits on the arrivals level. To get an idea of the costs, see
www.koeln-bonn-airport.de/parken-anreise/taxi.html

CAR HIRE offices are in terminal 2 on level 0:
www.koeln-bonn-airport.de/parken-anreise/mietwagen.html
By car it takes around 25 minutes to reach the city centre via autobahn A 59.

● **OVERLAND BUS:** a cheap way of reaching Cologne from other German cities and abroad is to take a long-distance bus. The new bus station is at the airport.

● **RAIL:** there are convenient rail connections from many European countries, with more than 1,300 trains from abroad and other German cities arriving daily in Cologne. Service hotline tel. 0180/6996633
www.bahn.de

Connections to the central station (Hauptbahnhof; *koeln-hbf.de*): local trains S 6, S 11, S 12 and S 13, trams 5,16 and 18 to the subway stations Dom/Hbf and Breslauer Platz, buses 132, 133, 250, 260 and 978 to Dom/Hbf.

TAXIS are on the right when leaving the station on the cathedral side; on the other side they stop at the north end of Breslauer Platz.

BICYCLES: there is a bike-hire station on Breslauer Platz, exit A, about 50 metres towards the river Rhine.
www.callabike-interaktiv.de

HIRE CARS: various companies, see rail information for Flinkster and in the passage opposite the travel centre Sixt, Europcar, Avis.

● CAR: Cologne is surrounded by an orbital highway from which ten highways radiate in all directions (A 1, A 3, A 4, A 57, A 59, A 555, A 559). For park and ride, see *www.kvb-koeln.de/german/ fahrplan/parkandride.html* Note that only vehicles with a green environmental sign for emissions class 4 may enter Cologne city centre.

BANKS

◆ All major German banks have branches in Cologne city centre (on Unter Sachsenhausen, Neumarkt, Hohenzollern- and Habsburgerring), open at the usual times, generally 8.30am-4pm.

ReiseBank Köln
· **Hauptbahnhof**
Tel. 0221/134403
◆ 7am-10pm
· **Cologne-Bonn Airport**
(terminal 1C, departures)
Tel. 02203/102918
◆ 7am-8pm

TICKET SALES

KölnTicket
Bischofsgartenstrasse 1
Tel. 0221/2801
www.koelnticket.de

Theaterkasse am Hansaring
Hansaring 64
Tel. 0221/9130116
www.theaterkasse.de

In Kaufhof department store
Hohe Strasse 1
Tel. 0221/2578811

Theaterkasse Rudolfplatz
Hohenzollernring 2
Tel. 0221/2582957
www.theaterkasse-rudolf-platz.de

In the subway passage on Neumarkt
Tel. 0221/2573842

EMERGENCY

Police tel. 110
Fire dept. tel. 112
Emergency doctor
Tel. 116117
Emergency dentist
Tel. 01805/986700
Emergency pharmacy:
www.aponet.de
Lost and found:
www.stadt-koeln.de/service/ adressen/fundbuero

PUBLIC TRANSPORT

Kölner Verkehrsbetriebe (KVB)
www.kvb-koeln.de
Timetables and fares
tel. 01803/504030
Tickets: customer centre on Neumarkt (subway)
◆ Mon-Fri 8am-8pm, Sat 8.30am-5pm

POST

Main post office in WDR-Arkaden
Breite Strasse 6–26
◆ Mon-Fri 9am-7pm, Sat 9am-2pm

CITY TOURS

KölnTourismus (tourist office)
Tel. 0221/346430
www.koelntourismus.de/ stadtfuehrungen/oeffentliche-fuehrungen.html

Domforum (cathedral)
Domkloster 3
Tel. 0221/92584730
www.domforum.de
◆ Mon-Fri 9.30am-6pm, Sat 9.30am-5pm, Sun 1-5pm

Inside Cologne
Bismarckstrasse 70
Tel. 0221/521977
www.insidecologne.de

Kölner Frauen-geschichtsverein (women's history)
Marienplatz 4
Tel. 0221/248265
www.frauengeschichts verein.de

RegioColonia e. V.
Marienplatz 4
Tel. 0221/9654595
www.regiocolonia.de

Segway Tour Köln
Tel. 0221/27260597
www.seg-tour-koeln.de

StattReisen Köln
Bürgerstrasse 4
Tel. 0221/7325113
www.stattreisen-koeln.de

Verein Kölner Stadt-führer e. V.
Schwalbacher Strasse 13
Tel. 0221/362914 and 01520/5119673
www.koelner-stadtfuehrer.de

TAXI

Tel. 0221/2882
or 19410

3 TIP The KölnCard gives you free trips on local public transport for either 24 or 48 hours and up to 50 per cent discount for services in the fields of art, culture and eating out. The KölnCard is on sale at the KölnTourismus Service Centre opposite the cathedral and from all ticket machines of the KVB and DB (rail operator), in many hotels/hostels and from a number of travel agents.
www.koelntourismus.de/ willkommen/ koelncard.html

Cologne's History

38 BC The Roman general Agrippa brings the Germanic Ubii tribe to the left bank of the Rhine and founds the Oppidum Ubiorum.

50 BC Emperor Claudius, at the prompting of his wife Agrippina, raises the status of the town, giving it the name Colonia Claudia Ara Agrippinensium, CCAA for short.

90 CCAA becomes capital of Lower Germany; the governor resides in the Praetorium.

c. 310 Emperor Constantine builds the military camp Divitia (Deutz today) on the right bank of the Rhine to secure the border and links it to the Roman town with a bridge.

c. 313 Maternus is the first named bishop of Cologne.

454 The Franks become rulers of the city.

c. 790 Charlemagne makes Cologne an archdiocese, headed by Archbishop Hildebold.

953 Emperor Otto I gives his brother, Archbishop Bruno of Cologne, the Duchy of Lorraine – putting religious and secular power in the same hands for the first time.

1164 Archbishop Rainald von Dassel brings the bones of the Three Magi to Cologne.

from 1180 Through the third extension of its boundaries, Cologne becomes the biggest city in the empire.

1248 Archbishop Konrad von Hochstaden lays the foundation stone of the new cathedral.

1288 Cologne's citizens get their political independence from the archbishop in the Battle of Worringen.

1388 The first municipal university in Germany is established in Cologne.

1396 The guilds of artisans issue a democratic constitution of the city and take power from the patrician families.

1424 After pogroms in the 14th century, the Jews are permanently expelled from the city.

1475 Cologne gains the status of a Free Imperial City.

1560 Building work on the cathedral is officially suspended.

1794 French revolutionary forces occupy Cologne and end its period as a Free Imperial City.

1802 Many churches are closed, all monasteries and religious foundations are dissolved.

1815 After the withdrawal of the French, Cologne and the Rhineland are given to Prussia at the Congress of Vienna.

1823 The first parade on Carnival Monday passes through Cologne.

1880 The cathedral is finally finished.

1917 to 1933 Konrad Adenauer is Lord Mayor of Cologne.

1938 In the pogrom night, all synagogues in Cologne are destroyed.

1945 American forces occupy Cologne, which is largely in ruins.

1948 The Ford factory produces its first Ford Taunus.

1972 Heinrich Böll is awarded the Nobel Prize for Literature.

1985 In the year of the Romanesque churches, Cologne celebrates the reconstruction of twelve important places of worship.

1999 A double summit of the EU and the G7 states is held in Cologne.

2001 The new Wallraf-Richartz-Museum is opened.

2007 Kolumba, the diocesan museum, is completed.

2010 Opening of the new Rautenstrauch-Joest-Museum.

2012 Renovation of the opera house by the architect Riphahn begins.

2015 The Rhine boulevard in Deutz is inaugurated.

Picture Credits
All photos by BKB Verlag except 1. FC Köln/photo Thomas Fähnrich 68 top, Amalia Ulman, Stock Images of War (Hospital), June 2015 © Stiftung Skulpturenpark Köln, 2016, photo: Axel Schneider 65 right, Art Cologne 43 top, U1 below right, BAP/Markus-Hausschild 25 centre, BB Promotion GmbH/© Nilz Böhme 25 top, BRAINPOOL TV GmbH 61 top, c/o pop 59 centre, Deutsche Kultur & Sport Marketing GmbH 41 centre, Fotolia U8, Gürzenich-Orchester Köln 60 top, Hänneschen-Theater – Puppenspiele der Stadt Köln 18 centre, Hopper St. Antonius 50 top, Johann Maria Farina/CC BY-Sat 4.0 16, Kölner Lichter® 23, 58 centre, 70 right, Koelnmesse U1 top, 1, 21 top, 67 top, KOLUMBA/Kunstmuseum des Erzbistums Köln 32 top, KOMED im MediaPark GmbH 63 below, lit.COLOGNE GmbH 62 centre, Little Link/Cocktailkunst GmbH 58 top, Maibeck/ © SPEISERAUM Fotografie 52 below, Miss Paepki 49, Museum für Angewandte Kunst/ Rheinisches Bildarchiv Köln (RBA) 2008, photo: Maria Luckey 64 top, Museum Ludwig/ Rheinisches Bildarchiv Köln/Britta Schlier 46 top, 47 below, © MUSICAL DOME KÖLN 24 top, Oper Köln 60 top, 63 top, Privatbrauerei Gaffel 56 below, 57 below, Rhine Connection Gastronomie-und Veranstaltungs-GmbH 26 below, Schokoladenmuseum Köln 41 top, Stadtgarten 24 below, 55 below, Stadt Köln 15 below, Theater der Keller/ © MEYER ORIGINALS 61 below, Törtchen Törtchen 34 below, Wallraf-Richartz-Museum & Fondation Corboud 45, 48 centre, Zoologischer Garten Köln/Rolf Schlosser 51 below